Understanding Statistics

To view the *Understanding Statistics* lecture
series, **head here:**

**www.libertarianism.org/guides/
understanding-statistics**

Understanding Statistics

AN INTRODUCTION

Antony Davies

CATO INSTITUTE
WASHINGTON, D.C.

Paperback ISBN: 978-1-944424-35-0
eBook ISBN: 978-1-944424-36-7

Library of Congress Cataloging-in-Publication Data available.

Printed in the United States of America.

CATO INSTITUTE
1000 Massachusetts Avenue, N.W.
Washington, D.C. 20001
www.cato.org

CONTENTS

Introduction: Why We Think Statistics Is Difficult

This book is an introduction to *statistics*, not an introduction to *statistical analysis*. Statistical analysis is about performing statistical calculations and estimating probabilities. This book is for someone who wants to learn how to interpret the results of statistical analyses. Think of it like the difference between being able to read a book and being able to write a book. One doesn't have to be an author to enjoy reading. Similarly, one does not need to know how to perform statistical analysis to understand statistics. From a practical perspective, understanding statistics can be as important as being able to perform statistical analysis.

Statistical analysis is a mathematical endeavor. Therefore, the formulation of the questions, the tools used in performing analyses, and the results those analyses yield are all expressed in mathematical language. Translating the mathematical results into English is fraught with difficulty. Understanding statistics helps to mitigate the errors that arise from inexact translations. For example, an analyst might discover a statistically positive relationship between the minimum wage and unemployment. But that finding doesn't *necessarily* mean that a noticeable increase in the unemployment rate will follow an increase in the minimum wage. Whether the relationship is noticeable depends on several factors, such as: (1) the magnitude of the minimum wage increase; (2) the difference between the proposed minimum wage and the current average hourly wage rate; (3) which sectors of the economy are growing and contracting; and (4) whether by "unemployment rate" we mean the unemployment rate in general, or the unemployment rate for hourly workers, or the unemployment rate for hourly entry-level workers, or the unemployment rate for hourly, entry-level, unskilled workers. Whereas measuring the effect of a minimum wage hike on the unemployment rate requires knowledge of *statistical analysis*, understanding the nuances of the results that the analysis yields requires knowledge of *statistics*.

Many children learn simple addition and subtraction by locating numbers on a number line. For example, to add three and two, you first find three on the number line and then move two places to the right. That puts you at five—three plus two is five. This is a useful way for children to begin to understand numbers and arithmetic. Unfortunately, most of us keep this model in our heads as adults—and this model is antithetical to understanding statistics. In statistics, things aren't as nicely arranged and well-behaved as they are on a number line. In statistics, things move around and vibrate in random ways, leading to all sorts of very real but counterintuitive results. For example, suppose your car can travel 30 miles (on average) on a gallon of regular gas and 36 miles (on average) on a gallon of premium gas. If you put one gallon of regular gas and one gallon of premium gas in your tank, how many miles will you travel? If you answered "66," you are suffering from the erroneous "number line" view of the world. The correct answer is "I don't know." You do know that you will travel 66 miles *on average*, but that's very different from saying you will travel 66 miles. The miles you can travel on a gallon of gas is a random variable. On average, it is 30 miles for regular gas. And, on average, it is 36 miles for premium gas. But those numbers

3

Figure 1
How We Imagine Measurements Work

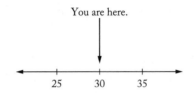

are only averages. On any given trip, you may get better or worse gas mileage depending on how much weight is in the car, whether the engine is well tuned, how much air pressure is in the tires, and many other factors. The mileage you get from a gallon of gas is not a fixed point on a number line (as in Figure 1). It is a cloud of points that vibrate around a common center (as in Figure 2). That common center is the **mean** (which is the technical name for "average"). The degree to which the cloud of points is spread out is called the **standard deviation** (an alternate measure is the **variance**).

Figure 2
How Measurements Actually Work

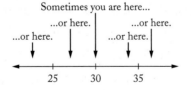

It turns out that most phenomena we deal with on a daily basis are more accurately represented as vibrating clouds rather than as points on a number line. For example, what time do you get up in the morning on a work day? If you answered something like "6:00 a.m.," you are thinking in number-line mode. You might set your alarm for 6:00 a.m. But, depending on how tired you are, whether you happened to wake up early, whether your power went out, how accurate your clock is, and many other factors, you won't get up at exactly 6:00:00.00 a.m. You'll get up a little earlier some days and a little later other days. The time you get up is not a point on the number line. It is a cloud that vibrates around 6:00 a.m. For more organized and punctual people, that cloud will have a smaller standard deviation—it will vibrate by a lesser amount around 6:00 a.m. For less organized people, that cloud may have a larger standard deviation. This mistaken view of measures as static points on a number line contributes to a mistaken view of statistical relationships.

Is four greater than three? Yes, four is always greater than three. That's because the relationship between four and three is **deterministic**. The fact that four and three have fixed locations on the number line is what makes the relationship between them deterministic. Deterministic relationships are always true. If you ever find a single example in which

5

a supposedly deterministic relationship is not true, you have proven that the relationship does not exist. For example, the relationship between air speed and air pressure is deterministic. Other things equal, the faster air flows, the lower the pressure it exerts. Every time. We call this Bernoulli's law. We rely on the fact that the relationship between air speed and air pressure is deterministic every time we fly because that relationship is what keeps airplanes in the air. If you ever find just a single example in which increased air speed does not accompany decreased air pressure (other things remaining unchanged), then you have disproved Bernoulli's law. To be a law, the relationship must apply every single time. That is, the relationship must be deterministic.

In contrast, economic relationships are **stochastic**. Stochastic relationships apply on average or, "in the **aggregate**" (i.e., in total), but may or may not apply in individual cases. For example, domestic dogs are bigger than domestic cats in a stochastic sense, not a deterministic one. By this we mean that the average dog is bigger than the average house cat, but there are individual exceptions. A full grown Toy Fox Terrier weighs between 3 and 9 pounds, while a full-grown Maine Coon cat weighs between 15 and 35 pounds. Finding an exception to a stochastic relationship does not disprove the relationship because stochastic relationships hold on average even if not in every particular case. The higher a person's hourly wage, the more hours per day the hourly worker will be willing to work. We call this relationship "labor supply." It is true in a stochastic sense: on average, that's what theory predicts and it's what we actually observe. However, you may be able to find a specific person who, after receiving an increase in his hourly wage, chooses to work fewer hours. The specific example doesn't invalidate the principle because the principle is stochastic. This is why we sometimes call economic laws "laws" (in scare quotes). Finding a counterexample to a stochastic relationship does not disprove the relationship. To disprove the relationship, one must demonstrate that the relationship does not hold on average, regardless of whether it holds in particular examples.

What does this discussion have to do with statistics? Statistical analysis (and **econometric analysis**—the application of advanced statistical analysis to economic data) provides a suite of tools for analyzing stochastic relationships. The tools are designed to distinguish relationships from background "noise." Think of the technology that characters in spy movies use to isolate a single voice from an audio recording of many voices in a crowd. That's what statistics and econometrics help us do. But instead of isolating a voice in a crowd, we are attempting to isolate a specific relationship against a background of other relationships and random events. For example, a company's quarterly sales are influenced by many factors, among them the price of its product, special discounts it may be offering, consumers' incomes, the prices of competitors' products, the weather, the unemployment rate, people's expectations, and a host of other factors. Using statistical analysis, we can isolate the effect of changes in the price of the company's product on the company's sales, after filtering out the effects of the other factors.

People can rightly be accused of sloppy thinking when they inappropriately substitute anecdotes for data (or, more correctly, for statistics) because in doing so they have failed to recognize the difference between stochastic and deterministic relationships. Anecdotes are entertaining. Statistics are dry. Anecdotes tend to resonate better with listeners. Listeners remember anecdotes and better understand the story the anecdotes tell. When explaining deterministic relationships, anecdotes can be used in place of statistics, since in a deterministic relationship *every* example conforms to the relationship. If I want to demonstrate the relationship between mass and gravity, I can tell a story about how Byron Jones, who holds the world record for the standing long jump (12 ft., 2 ¾ in.), would be able to jump more than 70 feet on the moon because the moon's mass is much less than Earth's.

But, where stochastic relationships are concerned, anecdotes can't substitute for statistics because individual examples may confirm or may contradict the stochastic relationship. A story about a person who lost his job the day after the minimum wage rose is not evidence for the relationship between unemployment and wage controls. Conversely, a story about a person who never lost his job despite several increases in the minimum wage is not evidence against the relationship between unemployment and wage controls. The anecdotes are irrelevant because the relationship they are attempting to describe is stochastic. What matters is the *aggregation* of all the stories into statistics. When the minimum wage rises, some people will be hired, some will keep their jobs, and some will lose their jobs. To determine whether there is a relationship between unemployment and wage controls, we need to compare the total number who gained jobs with the total number who lost jobs, and then we need to control for factors other than the minimum wage that may have influenced employment. Examples of individual people who gained or lost jobs are irrelevant. That doesn't mean anecdotes have no role to play in explaining stochastic relationships. Rather, it shows that the appropriate role for anecdotes is in *illustrating* facts that the statistics present, not in *discerning* what those facts might be.

Before we delve into understanding what statistics are, let us begin with some common errors to avoid when dealing with statistics.

1

Common Errors

Be Careful When Translating Statistics into English

An oft-repeated criticism is that one can make statistics say anything. That's not correct. Statistics don't "say" anything at all. The person interpreting the statistics is doing the saying. The problem is that statistics exist in the language of mathematics. When we translate the mathematics into English, we introduce the possibility of error and misinterpretation—and the error can be the listener's fault as readily as the speaker's. For example, consider the following statistics (the dollar figures are adjusted for differences in cost of living and are converted to U.S. dollars):

Average per capita income in Eastern Europe
one generation ago = $3,400

Average per capita income in Asia
one generation ago = $1,600

These are statistical statements, and many people would accept the following sentence as an accurate translation of the statistics:

"A generation ago, Eastern Europeans' incomes exceeded Asians' incomes."

But that interpretation isn't correct. The population of Eastern Europe is around 100 million, whereas the population of Asia is around 4 billion. At an average of $3,400 each, Eastern Europeans earned a total of around $340 billion in income while, at an average of $1,600 each, Asians received a total of around $7 trillion in income—or about 20 times what the Eastern Europeans earned.[1]

A more refined translation might be:

"A generation ago, *individual* Eastern Europeans earned higher incomes than did *individual* Asians."

This interpretation isn't correct either because we only know average incomes. It is possible that some Eastern Europeans' incomes were much less than the $3,400 average for Eastern Europe, and it is possible that some Asians' incomes were much greater than the $1,600 average for Asia. Unless every Eastern European were earning exactly $3,400 and every Asian were earning exactly $1,600, we could not say that individual Eastern Europeans earned more than did individual Asians.

The statistics we have tell us only the average per capita income. We have no idea how typical this average was for individual people. For example, it's possible that all Eastern Europeans earned approximately $3,400 plus or minus a few hundred dollars. Or, it is possible that most people earned nothing at all while a small number earned billions of dollars. In short, we don't know how much individual people's incomes are *dispersed* around the average. We know the random variable's average, but we don't know its standard deviation.

The media are quick to report averages, but they rarely report standard deviations. Yet the average alone doesn't tell us nearly as much as the average and standard deviation together. Roughly speaking, a standard deviation measures the average amount by which individual observations differ from the average. For example: Randomly select 100 high school students and weigh each one. Examine by how much the weights of the individual students differ from the average weight for the set of 100 students. Then randomly select 100 professional jockeys and weigh each one. Examine by how much the weights of the individual jockeys differ from the average weight for the set of 100 jockeys. The weights of the individual jockeys will all likely be rather close to the average weight for all the jockeys. In contrast, the weights of the individual students will likely vary from the average for all the students by a larger amount. In technical language, we say that the standard deviation of the jockeys' weights is lower and the standard deviation of the students' weights is higher.

Depending on the circumstances, the standard deviation of a random variable can be just as important as the random variable's average. For example, the mean temperature on the moon is around 5 degrees (Fahrenheit). The mean temperature in Fairbanks, Alaska, in February is about −2 degrees. Based on those means, it would appear that the moon's temperature is more hospitable than that of Fairbanks in winter. But we're ignoring the standard deviation. Fairbanks's February temperatures vary from a typical high of 10 degrees to a typical low of −13 degrees, putting the standard deviation somewhere around 12 degrees. In other words, Fairbanks's daily temperature fluctuates around its mean of −2 degrees by about 12 degrees up or down, on average. But the standard deviation of temperatures on the moon is around 250 degrees, meaning that a typical high on the moon is 255 degrees and a typical low is −245 degrees. It turns out that the standard deviation is incredibly important. If we compare mean temperatures, surviving on the moon seems a little easier than surviving a Fairbanks winter. But when we look at the standard deviations, we see that we wouldn't survive even a single day under the moon's temperatures. In this case, it's the temperature extremes, not the means, that are deadly.

Beware of Correlation

Even people not schooled in statistical analysis know that correlation is not causation. Just because two things move together doesn't mean that one causes the other. But it's more complicated than the simple phrase, "correlation isn't causation."

Figure 3 shows the number of sunspots (darker line) in each year from 1960 through 1980, and the number of Republicans in the U.S. Senate one year later (lighter line). Notice that the two data sets are correlated (i.e., they move together). When the number of sunspots declines, the number of Republicans in the Senate one year later falls. When the number of sunspots increases, the number of Republicans in the Senate one year later rises. Of course, it's unlikely that sunspots affect elections, so what we're seeing is an example of correlation without causation. Two things can be correlated because one causes the other, but they can also be correlated because, by

Figure 3
Sunspots and Republicans in the Senate, 1960–1980

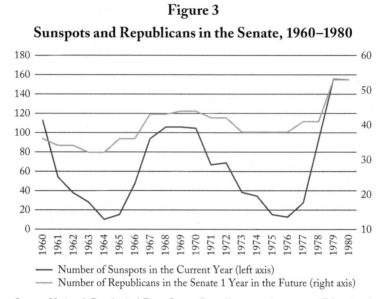

— Number of Sunspots in the Current Year (left axis)
— Number of Republicans in the Senate 1 Year in the Future (right axis)

Source: National Geophysical Data Center (http://www.sws.bom.gov.au/Educational
/2/3/6); U.S. Senate, "Party Division" (www.senate.gov/pagelayout/history/one_item
_and_teasers/partydiv.htm).

random chance, they happen to move in the same direction. Since you were born, you've gotten taller. Also, since you were born, the stock market has gone up in value. Changes in your height don't cause changes in the stock market, and changes in the stock market don't cause changes in your height. The two phenomena are correlated but not causally related.

Now, you might argue that, even though there is no causal relationship between sunspots and Republican senators, had you known about this correlation, you could have used it to predict election results. After all, if your goal is to predict an election, all you care about is *that* sunspots predict Republicans in the Senate—the *why* doesn't matter. The problem is that you're seeing the data in hindsight. In 1960, no one could make use of the correlation shown in Figure 3 because the data shown on the chart didn't exist. Now, by 1970, the data in the left half of the chart existed. But, if you were an election analyst in 1970 and saw the left half of this chart, you might have said something like, "Well, sunspots and Republicans do appear to move together, but we're only seeing 10 years here. And even then, it's a single down followed by a single up. Who knows whether this pattern is going to continue?" In short, in 1970, if you saw the left half of this chart, you probably would not have been sufficiently convinced to actually start using sunspots as an election predictor.

But, by 1980, you would have had the whole chart in front of you. You would have seen that sunspots correctly predicted elections for the past 20 years. Not only that, they predicted elections through a period of Republican losses (1960–1964), then Republican gains (1964–1969), then losses (1969–1976), then gains again (1976–1980). So, by 1980, you would probably have felt more confident about using sunspots to predict elections. You would have known that there couldn't

17

be a causal relationship, but nonetheless, if you had been using sunspots as predictors over the previous 20 years, you would have been able to predict election results very well.

And here's the problem with correlation in the absence of causation. Without causation, the correlation is simply due to random chance. Because the correlation is due to random chance, you never know when the correlation will disappear. It turns out that the correlation between sunspots and Republican victories disappeared around 1980—about the same time you would have started becoming comfortable with relying on sunspots as a predictor.

Figure 4 shows sunspots and Republicans in the Senate from 1981 through 2005. Notice that the correlation has vanished. In fact, from 1987 through 1999, sunspots moved in the *opposite* direction of the number of Republicans in the Senate.

Random correlation is the basis for a well-known stock scam.[2] An investment adviser emails 200,000 people (group A) telling them that the stock market will rise the next day, and another 200,000 people (group B) telling them that the stock market will fall the next day. The stock market actually rises, so the investment adviser takes group A and splits it in half. To 100,000 people (group C) he emails a prediction that the stock market will rise the next day. To the other 100,000 (group D)

Figure 4

Sunspots and Republicans in the Senate, 1981–2005

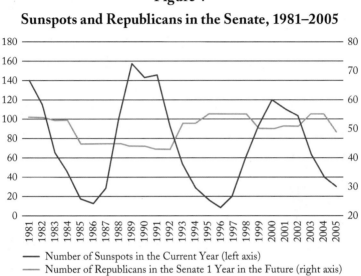

— Number of Sunspots in the Current Year (left axis)
— Number of Republicans in the Senate 1 Year in the Future (right axis)

Source: National Geophysical Data Center (http://www.sws.bom.gov.au/Educational /2/3/6); U.S. Senate, "Party Division" (www.senate.gov/pagelayout/history/one_item _and_teasers/partydiv.htm).

he emails a prediction that the stock market will fall the next day. The stock market actually falls, so the investment adviser takes group D and splits it in half. To 50,000 people (group E) he emails a prediction that the stock market will rise the next day. To the other 50,000 (group F) he emails a prediction that the stock market will fall the next day. The stock market actually falls. Now the investor emails the people in group F and says that he correctly predicted stock market movements in each of the past three days. If they'd like to continue receiving his predictions, they can pay him $20 each.

For those 50,000 people, the investor did correctly predict stock market movements three days in a row. But, he did so by random chance. His predictions were correlated with the stock market but, since there is no causality, there is no reason to believe that his predictions will continue to be correlated with the stock market.

Beware of Causation

Even if we correctly identify two phenomena as causal, we can mischaracterize the nature of causality. Every morning, you set your alarm. And every morning, the sun rises. The two events are causally related. But, it isn't your alarm clock causing the sun to rise. Rather, your anticipation of the sun rising causes you to set your alarm. Mischaracterizing causality in the wrong direction is called **reverse causality**. States with clean air and little pollen tend to have more asthma sufferers. The cleanliness of the air and the asthma rate are causally related. But it's not because clean air causes asthma. The causality runs in the other direction: asthma sufferers tend to move to states that have cleaner air.

Another mischaracterization of causality is the **third variable effect**. The third variable effect (also called a **confound**) occurs when two phenomena are causally related, yet neither causes the other. Instead, both are caused by a third phenomenon. For example, communities with more churches, on average, also experience more crimes. But crimes do not cause churches and churches do not cause crimes. Rather, both the number of churches and the number of crimes are caused by population size.

Although correlation is not causation, with rare exceptions, the absence of correlation is the absence of causation.[3] Figure 5 shows the most recent data for 113 reporting countries on

Figure 5
Economic Freedom Index and Global Peace Index
for 113 Countries, 2014 and 2017

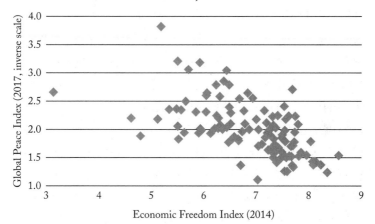

Economic Freedom Index (2014)

Source: Global Peace Index, Institute for Economics and Peace (http://visionof humanity.org/app/uploads/2017/06/GPI17-Report.pdf); Economic Freedom of the World, Fraser Institute (https://www.fraserinstitute.org/economic-freedom/dataset).

the economic freedom index (a measure of how free people are to make economic choices for themselves—a higher score means the country is more free) compared with the global peace index (a measure of the extent to which a country's government employs violence—a lower score means the country is more peaceful). The data are correlated: on average, countries that are more economically free are also more peaceful. Correlation isn't causation, so the data do not tell us that more economic freedom *causes* more peace. However, the absence of correlation is the absence of causation, so the data do tell us that more economic freedom *does not cause* less peace.

Beware of Aggregation Bias

Aggregation is the combining of many data points into a single measure. It's often necessary to aggregate data to reduce **noise**, or randomness in the data. For example, if I ask you how much the typical American worker earns today, picking a worker at random is likely not going to yield a good answer. You might, by random chance, pick someone who earns nothing because he is unemployed, or someone who earns a lot because he is a successful entrepreneur, or someone who earns little because he's a full-time student. Noise in the data makes it possible that the person you randomly select will not be typical. The right way to answer the question is to randomly select many workers and then combine their earnings. The combining causes the randomly higher wages to cancel out with the randomly lower wages. What's left we can consider a "typical" worker's earnings.

Note that, when data are aggregated, the observations must be selected randomly. If the data are not selected randomly, rather than the noise being smoothed out, the aggregated result becomes biased. In the extremely close 2000 presidential election, a problem arose because many Florida voters did not mark their ballots correctly. Florida used voting machines to count the ballots. If a voter didn't punch the holes on the ballot correctly, the voting machine couldn't read the ballot and so the voter's vote was declared "invalid." But, in many cases, manual inspection of the ballot would clearly reveal for whom the ballot was cast. So, if the ballots were recounted manually, many of the formerly invalid ballots would no longer be invalid. If the invalid ballots were randomly distributed among Republican and Democratic voters, the invalid ballots would simply be noise and it likely would not have mattered whether they were counted. So long as many valid ballots were counted, the noise of the invalid ballots would get drowned out. Nevertheless, both candidates called for manual recounts. Why? Because each hoped to obtain a *nonrandom* set of ballots. The Democratic candidate wanted manual recounts, but only in voting districts that were heavily Democratic. Similarly, the Republican candidate wanted manual recounts but only in districts that were heavily Republican. What the candidates were trying to do was obtain a *nonrandom* vote count that was biased in their favor.

When data are selected randomly, aggregation can drown out random noise in the data. But aggregation comes at a cost in that it can hide important information. For example, the lighter line in Figure 6 shows the median worker's (annualized) weekly wage and salary from 1979 through 2016 (adjusted for inflation).[4] The line fluctuates a little but is basically horizontal. This result is the basis for the argument that middle-class wages have stagnated. We obtain the line by finding the median (or "middle") worker's income in each year. This is a type of aggregation. So, in 1979, the middle worker earned about $42,000 in compensation (wages plus employer-paid benefits). And in 2016, the middle worker earned about $44,000.

Aggregation hides an important fact: the middle worker in each year is not the same worker. As the years go by, workers' wages rise as those workers obtain more skills, experience, and education. And new workers enter the workforce at starting-level wages. What we really want to know is what has happened to the same workers over time.

Figure 6
Median Worker Compensation Compared with Compensation over Median Career, 1979–2016, in 2017 Dollars

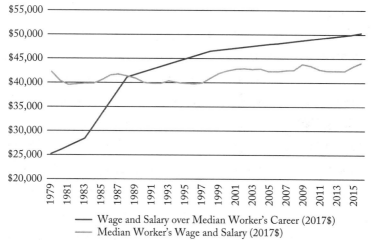

———— Wage and Salary over Median Worker's Career (2017$)
———— Median Worker's Wage and Salary (2017$)

Source: Current Population Survey, Bureau of Labor Statistics (https://www.bls.gov/cps/cpswktabs.htm, https://www.bls.gov/webapps/legacy/cpswktab3.htm).

The problem is clearer if we think of ages instead of wages. Consider a thought experiment: Suppose that in 2000, the median American was 37 years old, and that in 2010, the median American was 37 years old. Should we conclude that Americans didn't age from 2000 to 2010? Of course not. All Americans aged over this period. What did happen was that each year old people died (and so we stopped counting their high ages in our age calculations) and new people were born (each of whom starts with an age of zero). Although everyone got older, the makeup of the group we were looking at shifted such that the median age remained unchanged. The same is true with wages.

The darker line in Figure 6 shows the wage and salary for the median worker who was 16 years old in 1979.[5] It rises with each passing year because the median person in the age cohort earns more money because of increased education and job experience over time. The darker line is like tracking the median age of people born in a single year. Over time, those people will age. The lighter line is like tracking the median age of all people. That can remain constant even though each person is aging, because new young people are born and existing old people die. In this case, people at the end of their careers who are earning more money retire and so are no longer counted. Meanwhile, new people enter the workforce at starting-level wages.

Where the question of wage stagnation is concerned, it is the darker line we should be examining. What matters is how workers' incomes change over their careers, not what the median income of all workers over time is. What we see is that the median worker's compensation rose steadily from 1979 through 2016. Over that 38-year span, the median worker's purchasing power doubled.

Data showing income inequality in the United States are also subject to aggregation bias. For example, Figure 7 shows that, from 1995 to 2015, the poorest 20 percent of Americans went from earning 3.7 percent of all household income earned in the country to 3.1 percent. The data appear to show that the poor are getting poorer. But to arrive at these numbers, we've aggregated the poor in 1995 into a single number and then compared that with another aggregation of the poor in 2015.

Figure 7
Shares of Incomes Going to the Lowest and Highest Income Quintiles

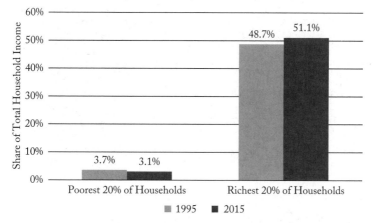

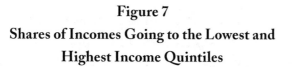

Source: Tax Policy Center (http://www.taxpolicycenter.org/statistics/household -income-quintiles)

Aggregation hides the fact that "the poor" in 2015 are not necessarily the same people who were "the poor" in 1995. In fact, if we apply the exact same calculations that produced this chart to age instead of income, we get Figure 8.

Figure 8 shows that, in 1990, the youngest 20 percent of Americans had an average age of 6.5 years. But in 2010, the youngest 20 percent of Americans had an average age of 7.2 years. Applying the same reasoning here that we applied

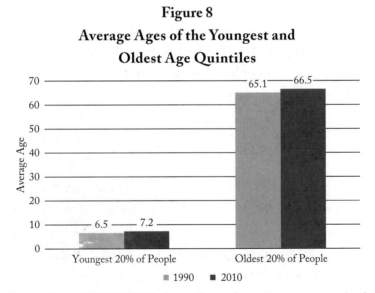

Figure 8

Average Ages of the Youngest and Oldest Age Quintiles

Source: Census 2000 Brief, U.S. Census Bureau (https://www.census.gov/prod/2001pubs/c2kbr01-12.pdf), Census 2010 Brief, U.S. Census Bureau (https://www.census.gov/prod/cen2010/briefs/c2010br-03.pdf).

to incomes, we would have to conclude that, over the 20 years from 1990 to 2010, the youngest people aged less than a year.

But clearly, that's not right. *Although every single young person aged 20 years from 1990 to 2010, the average age of young people increased by only 8 months.* How is this possible? The people who comprised the youngest 20 percent in 1990 were not necessarily the same people who comprised the youngest 20 percent in 2010. Over those decades, most of the people in the youngest 20 percent grew old enough to no longer be among the youngest 20 percent. And, over those decades, new people were born. In short, the "youngest 20 percent" in 2010 were not the same people as the "youngest 20 percent" in 1990, and so the two groups can't be directly compared.

One might be tempted to say that none of this matters. If the poorest 20 percent of Americans earn only 3.1 percent of the income, then we have a problem. The unspoken assumption is that, by "income," we mean income earned over the course of the past calendar year. But there is nothing special about a calendar year. Suppose we redefined "income" to mean "income earned over the course of the past week." Most people are paid biweekly, which means that over the course of a single week about half of us get paid and the other half don't. So, over the course of a single week, 100 percent of the income goes to 50 percent of the workers while zero percent of the income goes to the other 50 percent of the workers. The example is silly in that measuring income over only a week is too restrictive. But measuring income over the course of a calendar year can also be too restrictive. For example, a year is far too short a span to measure adequately the income of a college student who currently earns less than a poverty-line income but who is training to be a petrochemical engineer with a starting salary of over $100,000. Altering the time span we are examining dramatically alters the inequality measure we obtain.

The most accurate way to measure income inequality is across the span of a person's career. The Pew Economic Mobility Project did this, though with families rather than individuals. Researchers measured the average incomes of families in each income quintile and then went back a generation later and measured the incomes of those families' children.[6] Their results are shown in Figure 9.

The researchers found that, one generation later, the children born into the poorest families were earning twice (in inflation-adjusted terms) what their parents had been earning, while the children born into the richest families were earning the same as what their parents had earned. These data suggest that, when we look across generations, the poor are getting richer faster than the rich are getting richer.

Figure 9
Incomes of Families, by Quintile

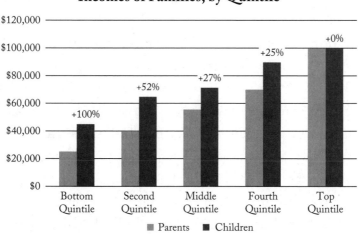

Source: Economic Mobility Project, "Economic Mobility of the States," Pew Center on the States, Washington, 2012.
Note: Figures are in 2006 dollars.

Be Careful That You're Measuring What You Think You're Measuring

Something odd happened in labor markets in 2013. From the third quarter to the fourth quarter, the unemployment rate fell from 7.2 percent to 7.0 percent. That was good news, of course, because it meant that more Americans were working. Except that it didn't. There were 82,000 fewer Americans working in the fourth quarter of 2013 than in the third quarter. How could the unemployment rate fall yet fewer

31

Americans be working? The answer lies in the definition of "unemployment"—it doesn't measure what many people think it measures.

Most people equate the **unemployment rate** with jobs. When unemployment is up, jobs are down, and vice versa. But that isn't necessarily true, and it wasn't true at the end of 2013. The reason is that a person can be categorized not only as "employed" or "unemployed," but also as **nonemployed**. A nonemployed person is one who doesn't have a job and isn't looking for one.[7] For example, full-time students, retired people, and homemakers are all classified as nonemployed. The **labor force** is the sum of employed and unemployed people. The nonemployed are not part of the labor force. When economists talk about the unemployment rate, what they mean is the number of unemployed people as a fraction of the labor force.

So what? Consider a simple case. Suppose we have a society composed of 5 million people, with 4.7 million of those employed and 0.3 million unemployed. The labor force is 5 million, and the unemployment rate is 6 percent (0.3 million/5 million).[8] Now, suppose 0.1 million of these people have been unemployed for so long that they give up hope of finding a job. We call these people **discouraged workers**. If jobs came along, they'd take them. But they've been fruitlessly searching for so long that they don't see the sense in actively looking anymore. Discouraged workers are not counted as part of the labor force.

What happens when these 0.1 million people drop out of the labor force? We are left with 4.7 million employed people, 0.2 million unemployed people, and 0.1 million nonemployed people. The labor force is 4.9 million (4.7 million employed plus 0.2 million unemployed), and the unemployment rate is 4.1 percent (0.2 million/4.9 million). Here's the interesting thing: the unemployment rate has fallen from 6 percent to 4.1 percent, yet the same number of people are working now as before (4.7 million). The disconnect between the unemployment rate and the number of jobs is due to the people moving from the unemployed to the nonemployed category.

And this is what happened in the latter part of 2013. Enough workers had been unemployed long enough to jump from the unemployed to the nonemployed category. As a result, the unemployment rate fell *and* the number of jobs declined.

An alternate measure is the employment rate. This is not simply 100 percent minus the unemployment rate. Whereas the unemployment rate is the number of unemployed people divided by the labor force, the **employment rate** is the number of employed divided by the population of working-age

33

adults. That one measure relies on the definition of "labor force" and the other doesn't presents pros and cons for each measure. The benefit of the *employment* rate is that, because it doesn't rely on defining who is and is not in the labor force, it is not affected by unemployed workers becoming discouraged. The benefit of the *unemployment* rate is that, because it does rely on defining who is and is not in the labor force, it ignores people who shouldn't be counted at all—such as retirees, full-time students, and people in prison.

Figure 10 shows the U.S. unemployment and employment rates for the four years following the start of the Great Recession. Notice the period from the fourth quarter of 2009 through the fourth quarter of 2011. The employment rate (the fraction of the working-age population that has a job) is flat, while the unemployment rate (the fraction of the labor force that does not have a job) is declining. For example, in the fourth quarter of 2009, the employment rate was 54.7 percent and the unemployment rate was 9.9 percent. By the fourth quarter of 2011, the unemployment rate had fallen to 8.6 percent, but the employment rate was the same 54.7 percent. The apparent improvement in the unemployment rate over these years was due to unemployed workers who became discouraged and dropped out of the labor force. The number of jobs (relative to the working-age population)

Figure 10
Unemployment Rate Compared with
Employment Rate, 2008–2011

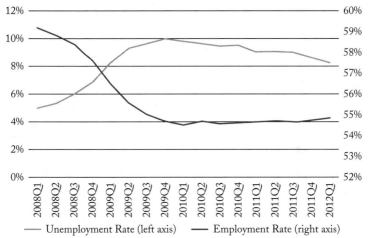

Source: Bureau of Labor Statistics, St. Louis Fed (https://fred.stlouisfed.org /series/UNRATE, https://fred.stlouisfed.org/series/EMRATIO).

did not change. This is a possible explanation for why, over this period, polls showed that Americans' confidence in the economy was not improving even though unemployment was falling.[9] The assessment of the "person on the street" was correct: the economy was not improving. The improvement in the unemployment numbers was not due to more people being employed but to fewer unemployed people being counted.

Inflation is another statistic that measures something different from what some people believe it measures. For example, some people point to a rise in the price of gas as an example of inflation. The price of gas is perhaps the most obvious of all prices because it changes frequently, it is prominently advertised, and gas is something many people buy often. But a rise in the price of gas is not an example of inflation. Inflation is the rise in the *average* price of goods consumers typically buy, not the rise in the price of a specific good. The Bureau of Labor Statistics (BLS) surveys urban consumers to determine what goods and services they typically buy, and in what quantities.[10] BLS calls this the "urban basket." Data collectors then visit or call thousands of stores to find what prices businesses are charging for the individual goods and services in the urban basket. Analysts combine those prices into a single index number, called the **Consumer Price Index for All Urban Consumers**, or CPI-U. BLS also calculates other average price measures on the basis of different baskets and prices. For example, the CPI-W is based on the basket and prices relevant to urban wage earners and clerical workers; the CPI-E is based on the basket and prices relevant to the elderly. Economists use the generic term "CPI" when referring to the CPI-U because this is the most general measure of consumer prices.

Consumer inflation is the growth rate in the CPI-U. For example, the CPI-U was 232.96 in 2013 and 236.71 in 2014.[11] From those figures, we can calculate that consumer inflation averaged 1.6 percent from 2013 to 2014.[12] Because this inflation measure is based on the average urban consumer's basket, it will be less meaningful for people whose consumptions differ markedly from the average urban consumer's consumption. For example, the elderly tend to spend a larger portion of their incomes on prescription drugs and a lesser portion on smart phones compared with the average urban consumer. Consequently, increases in the prices of prescription drugs will be more meaningful and increases in the prices of smart phones will be less meaningful to the elderly than to the general population. Similarly, the CPI measure that puts more emphasis on prescription drugs and less on smart phones (CPI-E) will better capture the prices that are relevant to the elderly.

Because the CPI represents the average of prices, some prices can be falling even though we are experiencing inflation. For example, the annual consumer inflation rate in 2014 was 0.8 percent.[13] Yet, over the same year, the price of gasoline fell 3.9 percent, and the price of computers fell 10 percent.[14] Conversely, the price of housing rose more than 5 percent.[15]

Another misleading statistic is **debt per GDP**. This is the size of a country's government's debt (also called the **public**

debt) relative to the size of the country's economy (measured by its gross domestic product). A government's debt is the amount of money a country's government has borrowed. People sometimes refer to this as the "country's" debt, as in "the United States' debt was almost $20 trillion in 2016." This short-hand way of referring to the public debt is technically incorrect. A country—which is composed of people, businesses, *and* the government—is not the same as the country's government. The public debt is money a country's government has borrowed, not money that the country's people or businesses have borrowed.

Debt per GDP is useful for comparing public debt across different governments. For example, as of 2016, Greece's public debt exceeded $350 billion (converted to U.S. dollars). That is an extremely small number compared with the United States' public debt. Comparing just the debts of the two countries' governments ($350 billion versus $20 trillion), Greece's public debt appears much lower. However, a comparison of the debts ignores the fact that the Greek government collects taxes from a $200 billion economy, whereas the U.S. government collects taxes from a $19 trillion economy. Relative to the sizes of their economies, Greece's public debt (175 percent of GDP) is much larger than the United States' public debt (105 percent of GDP).

Although debt per GDP is useful for comparing the magnitude of public debts across governments, it is less useful for measuring a government's ability to service its debt because the GDP doesn't belong to the government. GDP is (largely) the total income earned by businesses and people in a country and so belongs to those businesses and people. The GDP is not available to the government for paying its debts. A better measure of the government's ability to service its debt is debt per government receipts—public debt divided by the amount of money the government collects in a year from all sources combined. Federal debt per receipts in the United States is around 600 percent. That is, the federal government owes an amount of money that is about six times the amount of money it collects in taxes annually. For comparison, this is like a household with a $60,000 income being $360,000 in debt. Note that this is not like a $60,000 household having a $360,000 mortgage. A mortgage is a debt that is balanced by an asset—the value of the house. In 2016, the total value of all of the federal government's assets was around $3.3 trillion and the federal government's annual receipts totaled about the same $3.3 trillion.[16] Accounting for the government's assets, the government's financial situation is like that of a $60,000 household having a $60,000 mortgage on a $60,000 house and another $300,000 on its credit card.

These terms—unemployment rate, inflation rate, and debt per GDP—are just three examples of the importance of being extremely clear as to the definition of a statistic. Without this clarity, we can inadvertently say things that are not true. In addition to understanding a statistic's definition, one must also know how the data that feed into the statistic are collected. For example, BLS produces two employment estimates. One comes from a BLS survey of employers that asks how many workers those employers hired or let go. The other comes from a BLS survey of people that asks whether they found or lost jobs. In April 2012, the first survey indicated that employers added a net 115,000 jobs, while the second indicated that 169,000 Americans lost their jobs. Clearly, the two numbers are contradictory. Yet, both figures are estimates, so the correct statement is that the economy experienced something between 169,000 job losses and 115,000 job gains.[17]

Having been warned of common errors to avoid when dealing with statistics, we can now delve into statistics themselves. The place to begin is with probabilities. A probability—the likelihood of something happening—is the building block of statistics. Probabilities are what make things stochastic rather than deterministic.

2

What Are Probabilities?

A **probability** is the likelihood of an event occurring. Because it is simpler, we almost always talk in terms of certainties. We may say, "It will rain today," or "I will meet you at noon." But very few things are certain—our lives are composed almost entirely of probabilities. No matter how dark the sky, it is impossible to know for certain that it will rain. You may be so sure it will rain that you wear a raincoat and carry an umbrella. But you do not know for certain that it will rain. There is a probability, perhaps very small but definitely nonzero, that it will not rain. You may intend to meet someone at noon, but you cannot guarantee that you definitely will meet at noon. There is a nonzero probability that you'll have a flat tire on the way, or unexpected traffic will delay you, or your boss will suddenly give you an assignment that absolutely must be completed by the end of the day. Almost all the things we talk about as if they were certainties are actually probabilities. Statistics acknowledges the reality that almost all of life is probabilistic.

But although almost everything around us is probabilistic, we tend to think in terms of absolutes because absolutes are easier. It's easier to say, "We're going to need another gallon of milk before tomorrow," than to say, "There is a 95 percent chance that we will need another gallon of milk before tomorrow." Consequently, when we *do* turn our attention to probabilities, we are often mistaken about what we are seeing.

Observation Bias Leads to Misestimation of Probabilities

We commit **observation bias** when we erroneously believe that simply because we have personally observed something, that thing has a higher probability of occurring than does something we haven't observed.

For example, many people are afraid of flying. Our loved ones often admonish us to "call when the plane lands" so they will know we have arrived safely. But the most dangerous part of a plane trip (by far) is the drive to and from the airport. In 2013, almost 34,000 people died in automobile accidents in the United States.[18] According to the National Transportation Safety Board, the number of people killed in commercial flights in the United States in that same year was 5.[19] In other words, the average person who travels by car is almost 7,000 times more likely to die in a crash than is the average person who travels by plane. Of course, the probabilities are influenced by the length of the trip—the probability of death increases significantly with the length of a car trip, but hardly at all with the length of a plane trip (the bulk of the risk is in the takeoff and landing). But, someone who drives 30 miles every day is seven times more likely to die traveling than is someone who flies 500 miles every day.[20]

Similarly, some people spend a tremendous amount of energy worrying about so-called "assault rifles," yet the number of Americans killed annually by punches and kicks is twice the number killed by all types of rifles combined.[21]

So why do we worry about plane travel and rifles? The answer is observation bias. Our natural tendency is to think of ourselves and the things we encounter as "typical." Consequently, when we hear a news story about a plane crash, our natural tendency is to think that plane crashes are typical. But, typical events don't typically make the news. Car crashes occur in every city every day, so they don't appear on the news unless they are untypically horrific. *Extraordinary* events make the news. That means, on average, you can regard the news as a litany of things that are unlikely to harm you.

Repetition Can Cause (Indirect) Observation Bias

A form of observation bias comes from hearing something repeated over and over. For example, both the media and many people repeatedly say that the rich need to "pay their fair share of taxes." The phrase is repeated so often that many people (and sometimes even economists), absent any data, assume that the poor and middle class pay more taxes (or at least a greater percentage of their income in taxes) than do the rich. This is an "indirect" observation bias because the bias comes not from one's own observations but from what one perceives that others are observing. The cure for such biases is a look at the data. The Congressional Budget Office (CBO) tracks federal taxes received from and transfers paid to people in each of various income categories. The CBO breaks the population down into quintiles, and the top quintile into smaller gradations. For each income group, the CBO asks the following questions:

- How much income (from all sources—wages, interest, dividends, capital gains, etc.) did the average person earn?

- How much money did the average person pay in federal taxes (all taxes combined—income tax, payroll tax, corporate tax, capital gains tax, estate tax, etc.)?

44

The second number divided by the first number is the average **effective tax rate** for that income category. An effective tax rate is the tax rate a person actually pays, as opposed to a **statutory tax rate**, which—depending on deductions, tax credits, and other adjustments—the person may or may not actually pay. The average effective tax rate answers a simple question: when all the accounting and legal gymnastics are over, what fraction of all the money you received from all sources combined did you actually end up handing over to the Internal Revenue Service? (See Table 1.)

The data in Table 1 come from the CBO and are for 2011 (the latest year available; earlier years show roughly similar numbers). What's remarkable is the discrepancy between

Table 1. Effective Income Tax Rates, by Income Level

Income Category	Average Effective Income Tax Rate
Poorest 20%	1.9%
Next 20%	7.0%
Middle 20%	11.2%
Next 20%	15.2%
Richest 10% to 20%	18.6%
Richest 5% to 9%	21.1%
Richest 2% to 4%	24.3%
Richest 1%	29.0%

Source: Congressional Budget Office, "The Distribution of Household Income and Federal Taxes, 2011," November 2014 (Table 4).

the claim that the rich aren't paying their fair share and the numbers. The average person in the top 1 percent paid 29 percent of his income in taxes versus less than 2 percent for the average person in the bottom 20 percent. The question of whether those amounts are fair is left open because we haven't defined what "fair" is. However, the results fly in the face of the common claim that somehow the rich are paying less in taxes than are the poor. Not only are the rich paying more dollars than the poor (which we would expect), they are paying a greater fraction of their incomes than are the poor.[22]

Given Enough Opportunities, Even the Most Unlikely Event Is Guaranteed to Happen

The probability that a randomly selected person shares your birthday is 1 out of 365, or three-tenths of 1 percent. Phrased differently, the probability that a randomly selected person does *not* share your birthday is 99.7 percent. Put yourself in a room with two other people and the probability that neither of the other people will share your birthday is 99.7% × 99.7% = 99.5%. With a total of 11 people in the room, the probability that none of the other 10 people shares your birthday is 99.7% × 99.7% × 99.7% × . . . (10 times), or 97.3%. Even with 10 other people in the room, it's still almost certain that no one in the room shares your birthday. But, put 100 other people in the room and the probability of no one sharing your birthday is 76 percent. That's still rather high but no longer a near certainty. There's a 24 percent chance that at least one of the other 100 people shares your birthday.

Now, you might think that, because there are 365 days in the year, if there are 365 other people in a room with you, one of them is guaranteed to share your birthday. But that's not the way probabilities work. It is possible (though extremely unlikely) that the other 365 people all have the same birthday and that it isn't yours. It is possible (and somewhat more likely) that none of the other 365 people have birthdays in the same month as yours. Because of random chance, having 365 people in a room does not mean that each of the days of the year is represented. In fact, with 365 other people in the room, the probability that at least one of them shares your birthday is just over 60 percent. In other words, even if there are 365 other people in the room, there's still about a 40 percent chance that none of them share your birthday. You've got to pack about 1,700 other people in the room before you get a 99 percent chance that at least one of the other people shares your birthday.

The probability that a dangerously large asteroid will strike the Earth within the next year is 0.0003 percent, or, equivalently, the probability of *not* being struck is

99.9997 percent. A probability that high is a virtual certainty. You are safe assuming that it simply won't happen. This year. But allow enough years to pass, and the probability goes from nearly zero to nearly one. The probability that at least one dangerously large asteroid will hit the Earth within the next 10,000 years is 3 percent—still small enough to ignore. But the probability of such an asteroid hitting the Earth within the next 100,000 years is almost 30 percent, and within the next million years, 96 percent.

The moral of the story is this: even though the probability of an event is extremely small, if you try enough times, the event will happen.

On July 25, 2000, a Concorde supersonic jet crashed in France. It was the first time in its history that a Concorde had crashed. Prior to this single event, Concorde could claim a perfect safety record. By the same date, a total of 10 Boeing 737s had crashed. Yet officials grounded the entire fleet of Concordes while allowing Boeings to continue to fly. Why? Looking at the raw numbers, the 737s appear to be more dangerous planes.

But we're forgetting that even low-probability events— given enough opportunities—are guaranteed to happen. By July 25, 2000, Boeing 737s had accumulated a total of 31 million flights worldwide.[23] Concordes had accumulated a total of 80,000 flights. Considering the historical record, that single crash took the estimated probability of a given Concorde crashing from 0 percent (0 out of 80,000) to 0.001 percent (1 out of 80,000). That seems like an extremely small crash probability. But compare it to the Boeing 737s. At 10 crashes out of 31 million flights, the estimated probability of a given Boeing 737 crashing was 0.00003 percent. That single crash made Concorde's probability of crashing 33 times that of Boeing. The reason Boeing had 10 crashes, despite the probability of a given crash being incredibly low, is that Boeings had flown (literally) millions of times. No matter how small the probability of an event is, as long as the probability isn't zero, the event is guaranteed to occur if you try enough times.

Common Misconceptions about Probabilities

In no particular order, and largely skipping proofs, here are some commonly misunderstood facts about probabilities:

1. *The number of options doesn't determine the probability of each option occurring.*

   Just because there are two options doesn't mean that the probability of each of them occurring is 50 percent. Tell someone that a bowling ball rolling down a lane will either break left or break right, then ask the person

UNDERSTANDING STATISTICS: AN INTRODUCTION

what is the probability that the ball will break left. Most people will answer, "50 percent," and when you ask them to defend their answer, they'll say, "because there are two options." Regardless of whether the answer is correct, the reasoning is flawed. To demonstrate, tell the person that he is either alive or dead, and ask what is the probability that he is alive. Although there are two options, the probability is not 50 percent. Many people acquire this misconception because of how probabilities are taught. One of the first examples that statistics students encounter is a coin toss. There are two sides to the coin, and the probability of one of the sides landing up is one-half. In this example, it's easy to take away the erroneous conclusion that the probability is one-half because there are two sides. In fact, the number of sides has nothing to do with the probability. The probability is *not* determined by the number of sides but by the fact that the coin is evenly weighted.

2. *The probability of one improbable thing and many probable things occurring together is less than the probability of the improbable thing occurring alone.*

"Linda is 31 years old, single, outspoken, and very bright. She majored in philosophy. As a student, she was deeply

50

concerned with issues of discrimination and social justice and participated in antiwar demonstrations."[24]

Which is more likely: (a) Linda is a bank clerk, or
(b) Linda is a bank clerk and is active in the feminist
movement? Many people answer (b), though the correct answer is (a). The probability that (a) is correct is
the probability that Linda is a clerk. The probability
that (b) is correct is the probability that Linda is a clerk
and is a feminist—we call this a **joint probability**. By
definition, joint probabilities can't be greater than the
simple probabilities of which they are composed. For
example, if the probability of Linda's being a clerk is
50 percent and the probability of Linda's being a feminist is 90 percent, then the probability of Linda's being
a clerk *and* a feminist is 50% × 90% = 45%. That
result is less than the probability of her being a clerk.

3. *A percentage change and a percentage point change are very*
   different things.

On January 1, 2013, a popular payroll tax cut expired.
For the prior two years, the Social Security tax rate had
been 4.2 percent. On this date, the tax rate returned
to its earlier level of 6.2 percent. Politicians tried to
make light of the increase by saying that it was "only

a 2 percent increase." That is incorrect. An increase
from 4.2 percent to 6.2 percent is a two *percentage point*
increase. The difference in words is small, but the difference in dollars is quite large. Consider this example:
Increasing a tax rate from 1 percent to 2 percent dou-
bles the rate. That's a one percentage point increase,
but a 100 percent increase. Increasing a tax rate from 10
percent to 11 percent is a one percentage point increase,
but a 10 percent increase. The increase in the Social
Security tax rate from 4.2 percent to 6.2 percent was
a 48 percent increase.[25] Now this may all sound like
semantics, but notice the difference when we use the
tax rates to calculate your tax bill. Suppose you earned
$50,000 in wages. At a tax rate of 4.2 percent, you
would owe 4.2% × $50,000 = $2,100 in Social Security taxes. But, at a tax rate of 6.2 percent, you owe
6.2% × $50,000 = $3,100 in taxes. The $3,100 tax bill
is 48 percent greater than the $2,100 tax bill.

What's true of these tax rates is also true of probabilities. Suppose policymakers want to invest taxpayer
dollars in the development of a new cancer treatment
that promises to reduce deaths from a particular form
of cancer by 50 percent. That sounds like a tremendous improvement, and politicians would find it easy

to get voter support for such an investment. But suppose deaths from this particular form of cancer are rare—2 in 10,000. A 50 percent improvement would reduce deaths to 1 in 10,000. That is a one-tenth of one percentage point decline. Stating the improvement as a percentage point change rather than as a percentage change reveals that the absolute number of lives saved will be far fewer than the politician implied.

4. *When translated into English, conditional and joint probabilities sound similar, but they are not.*

The following is loosely based on an actual gender discrimination case involving officers of the New York Police Department (NYPD). Suppose the police department employs 1,200 officers, of whom 960 are men and 240 women. This year, the department promotes 288 men but only 72 women. Looking at the department as a whole, the probability of being a promoted female is 6 percent,[26] but the probability of being a promoted male is 24 percent.[27]

Conclusion: the department discriminates against women because the probability of being a promoted male is four times the probability of being a promoted female. Nothing is incorrect in the calculations or the translation of the calculations into English. Yet, the conclusion is incorrect.

The conclusion is incorrect because we are comparing the wrong measures. We are comparing the probability of being a promoted male to the probability of being a promoted female. We call these **joint probabilities** because each is the probability of more than one event—either the probability of being both a male and promoted, or the probability of being both a female and promoted. But joint probabilities aren't relevant here. What we want to know are **conditional probabilities**. Specifically: If I am a female, what is the probability of my being promoted? If I am a male, what is the probability of my being promoted? The confusing thing is that, when translated into English, the two types of probabilities sound similar:

- Joint probability: *The probability of a randomly selected officer's being a promoted female.*

- Conditional probability: *The probability of a randomly selected female officer's being promoted.*

Consider the hypothetical data in Table 2.

The probability of an officer being promoted *given* that the officer is a male is 30 percent.[28] The probability of an officer being promoted *given* that the officer

Table 2. NYPD Promotion of Males and Females

NYPD Officers	Promoted	Not Promoted	Total
Males	288	672	960
Females	72	168	240
Total	360	840	1,200

is a female is 30 percent.[29] Despite the fact that there are four times the number of promoted males as promoted females, there is no obvious gender discrimination because the conditional probabilities are the same for the two genders. In other words, the reason there are more promoted males than promoted females is not that males are more likely to be promoted. It is simply that there are more males than females on the force.

5. *The heart is a good tool for alerting us to potential concerns but a horrible tool for making decisions.*

In an apparent suicide in 2001, a teenage pilot flew a private airplane into a building in Florida. The teenager was one of 3 million teenagers taking Accutane, a popular drug for treating severe acne. That year, 37 teenage Accutane users committed suicide. Concluding that the drug was linked to the suicides, concerned parents and doctors called for the Food and Drug Administration (FDA) to ban the drug.

Out of 20 million teenagers in the United States that year, 2,000 committed suicide and only 37 of those were taking Accutane. Thirty-seven suicides might not seem like many, and it isn't clear that the Accutane was responsible for the suicides. However, there is a compelling argument that the ban is worthwhile even if it saves just one life. And this argument almost cost many other teenagers their lives.

The appropriate question here is not how many teenagers who committed suicide were taking Accutane, but what is the probability of a teenager committing suicide *given* that he is taking Accutane versus the probability of committing suicide *given* that he is not taking Accutane. The rough numbers are shown in Table 3.

Table 3. Suicide and Use of Accutane, 1982–2000

U.S. Population (ages 13 to 32)[30]	Used Accutane	Not Taking Accutane	Total
Committed suicide	37	34,337	34,374
Did not commit suicide	4,999,963	13,665,663	18,665,626
Total	5,000,000	13,700,000	18,700,000[31]

Source: "Estimating Accutane Use," Food and Drug Administration (https://www.fda.gov/ohrms/dockets/ac/00/backgrd/3639b1c_05.pdf); "Depression and Suicide in Patients Treated with Isotretinoin," *New England Journal of Medicine* (http://www.nejm.org/doi/full/10.1056 /NEJM200102083440616); Fatal Injury Reports, Centers for Disease Control (https://webappa.cdc.gov/sasweb/ncipc/mortrate.html).

According to the numbers, the probability of a person committing suicide given that he was taking Accutane was 0.0007 percent.[32] The probability of a person committing suicide given that he was not taking Accutane was 0.251 percent.[33]

In layman's terms, people who did not take Accutane experienced a greater probability of committing suicide than did people who did take Accutane.[34] Our well-meaning hearts went out to the 37 Accutane users who committed suicide but didn't see the 34,337 who also committed suicide but were not taking the drug. Fortunately, science and statistics prevailed and the FDA did not ban the drug. But it could easily have done so and, in our satisfaction about saving the 37, we might have overlooked the 34,337.

6. *Simpson's Paradox: What is true for the parts is not necessarily true for the whole.*[35]

Suppose you want to know whether a university hires males as readily as females. You start by looking at the individual departments within the university. The sociology department had five male applicants and eight female applicants. Of those, it hired one male and two females. (See Figure 11.)

Figure 11
Sociology Department Hiring

Sociology Department

Probability of male applicant being hired = 1 / 5 = 20%
Probability of female applicant being hired = 2 / 8 = 25%

You would conclude that there is no evidence that the sociology department favored men over women because it hired only 20 percent of the male applicants but 25 percent of the female applicants. That is, the probability of a sociology candidate's being hired given that the candidate is male is 20 percent, while the probability of a sociology candidate's being hired given that the candidate is female is 25 percent.

You move on to the math department and also find that the department favored women over men. Of eight male applicants, the department hired six, and of five female applicants, the department hired four. The probability of a math candidate's being hired given that the candidate is male is 75 percent, and the probability

Figure 12
Math Department Hiring

Math Department
Probability of male applicant being hired = 6 / 8 = 75%
Probability of female applicant being hired = 4 / 5 = 80%

of a math candidate's being hired given that the candidate is female is 80 percent. (See Figure 12.)

You are prepared to report that you have found no evidence of gender discrimination until it occurs to you to look at the total numbers for the two departments combined. And there, something fascinating emerges. The two departments together interviewed a total of 13 male candidates and hired seven. The two departments together interviewed a total of 13 female candidates and hired six. When you combine the two departments, you find that the probability of a candidate's being hired given that the candidate is male is 54 percent, whereas the probability of a candidate's being hired given that the candidate is female is only 46 percent.

Figure 13
Hiring in Both Departments Combined

Both Departments Combined

Probability of male applicant being hired = 7 / 13 = 54%
Probability of female applicant being hired = 6 / 13 = 46%

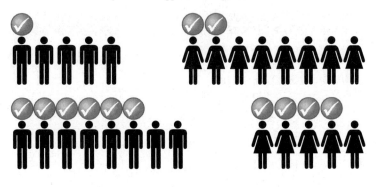

Paradoxically, you have found evidence that the departments, when combined as a whole, favored male candidates, even though each department separately favored female candidates. (See Figure 13.)

What is confusing here is that both statements are correct:

1. Each department is more likely to hire women than men.

2. The two departments combined are more likely to hire men than women.

The source of the paradox is that the sociology department hired very few applicants of either gender (3 out of 13, or

23 percent), whereas the math department hired most of its applicants (10 out of 13, or 77 percent). Because many women applied for the sociology positions but fewer applied for the math positions, the majority of the female applicants applied to the department that hired few of either gender. Conversely, the majority of the male applicants applied to the department that hired many of both genders. The result is that, in total, more men were hired than women.

The following three statements are all correct:

1. The probability of the sociology department hiring a female is greater than the probability of the sociology department hiring a male.

2. The probability of the math department hiring a female is greater than the probability of the math department hiring a male.

3. The probability of the two departments together hiring a female is less than the probability of the two departments together hiring a male.

What do we conclude? Is the university guilty of gender discrimination in hiring or not? The answer depends on whether you are concerned with discrimination in *process* or discrimination in *outcome*. Assuming that the male and female candidates were all equally well qualified, there is no discrimination in the hiring process. The sociology department hired a greater proportion of female applicants. The math department also hired a greater proportion of female applicants. In this example, the discrimination in outcome occurred not because of the employer's choices but because of the applicants' choices. A greater proportion of females chose to become sociologists while a lesser proportion chose to become mathematicians.

How Do We Know When Two Things Are Different?

You have two sticks. What do you do if you want to know which is longer? You measure each of them. The one with the greater measurement is the longer stick. Come back tomorrow and measure them again and (assuming no one has broken them and that you measured correctly both times) you'll get the same measurements as before. Each time you measure the sticks, you get the same measurements. You get the same measurements each time because the sticks' lengths are *deterministic*—barring any physical alteration of the sticks, the measurements don't change. So measuring is easy. Do it once and you're done.

But what if you want to know which of two cars gets better gas mileage, or which of two stocks yields a better return, or which of two states has greater unemployment? These phenomena (mileage, return, unemployment) are all *stochastic*. You won't get the same result each time you measure. Because you don't get the same result each time you measure, it is possible that successive measurements may be contradictory. Last month, Microsoft stock outperformed Amazon. This month, Amazon outperformed Microsoft. Determining which stock performs better is more complicated than simply comparing two measurements.

Comparing Unemployment Rates

For example, consider Pennsylvania's unemployment rate (shown in Figure 14). The rate doesn't remain constant. In March 2007, it was at a low of 4.3 percent. Three years later, it was at a high of 8.7 percent. If we want to know whether Pennsylvania's unemployment rate was greater than New York's unemployment rate, how would we compare the two measurements? We certainly can ask if Pennsylvania's unemployment rate *today* is greater than New York's unemployment rate *today*. We can even ask if Pennsylvania's *average* unemployment rate over the past decade is greater than New York's *average* unemployment over the past decade. But both of those questions miss an important nuance.

Figure 14
Pennsylvania Unemployment Rate, 2005–2015

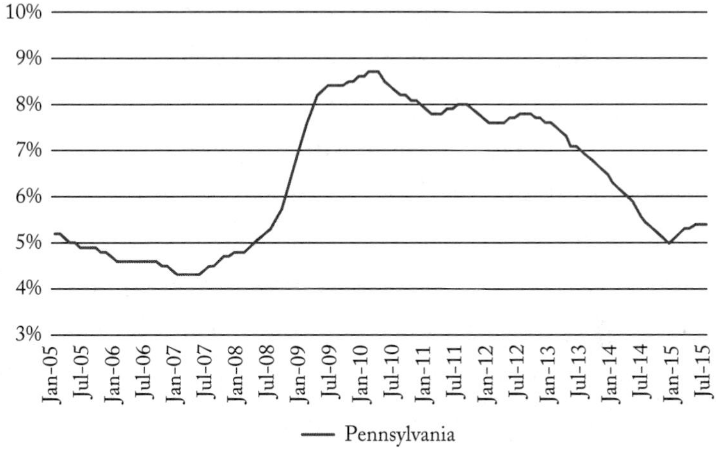

— Pennsylvania

Source: Bureau of Labor Statistics (https://data.bls.gov/timeseries/LASST42000 0000000003).

Pennsylvania's and New York's unemployment rates are stochastic—they are, at least partially, driven by random chance. The states' unemployment rates are driven by systemic factors such as their tax environments, infrastructure, people's educations, climates, and so on. But they are also driven by random, or stochastic, factors such as particular weather events, specific election outcomes, specific instances of corruption, and specific individuals moving into or out of the state, to name just a few. The stochastic events aren't the

65

result of anything systemic—they just happen randomly—yet they can influence the unemployment rate. But when we compare the unemployment rates, what we really want to compare are the systemic parts, not the stochastic parts.[36] For example, if I am choosing to start a business in one of those states and I want to know which has the lower unemployment rate, what I really care about are the systemic components of the unemployment rates because those systemic components will continue to affect the unemployment rates in the future. I don't care about the stochastic components because those random components will come and go unpredictably.

One thing I might do is compare the two states' unemployment rates over time as shown in Figure 15.

But this approach isn't entirely satisfying. There are some months in which the unemployment rate is lower in New York, other months when it is lower in Pennsylvania, and still others in which the two unemployment rates are the same.

To compare the two unemployment rates, we need more than just their averages. We also need their standard deviations. The standard deviation measures the degree to which the unemployment rate wanders away from its average. For example, Pennsylvania's average unemployment rate over this period is 6.4 percent while New York's is 6.7 percent.

Figure 15
Pennsylvania and New York Unemployment Rates,
2005–2015

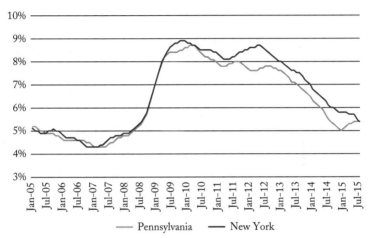

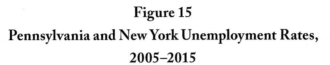

Source: Bureau of Labor Statistics (https://data.bls.gov/timeseries/LASST42000
0000000003, https://data.bls.gov/timeseries/LASST360000000000003).

Comparing just the average unemployment rates produces a
mental picture like the one in Figure 16.

If we look just at the averages, it appears that New York's
unemployment rate is (on average) larger than Pennsylvania's.
But that view ignores the fact that the two unemployment
rates wander. They aren't always 6.4 percent and 6.7 percent. They are only 6.4 percent and 6.7 percent *on average*.

Figure 16
Average Unemployment Rates in New York and Pennsylvania

Over this period, the standard deviation of Pennsylvania's unemployment rate is 1.5 percent. In other words, as Pennsylvania's unemployment rate wanders, from month to month, away from the average of 6.4 percent, it wanders an average distance of 1.5 percentage points. Looking at both the average and the standard deviation produces a very different picture of Pennsylvania's unemployment rate (Figure 17).

Figure 17 shows the average distance Pennsylvania's unemployment rate wanders away from its 6.4 percent average. This is not the entire range that Pennsylvania's unemployment rate

Figure 17
Average and Standard Deviation of
Unemployment Rate in Pennsylvania

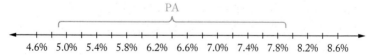

Figure 18
Average and Standard Deviation of
Unemployment Rate in New York

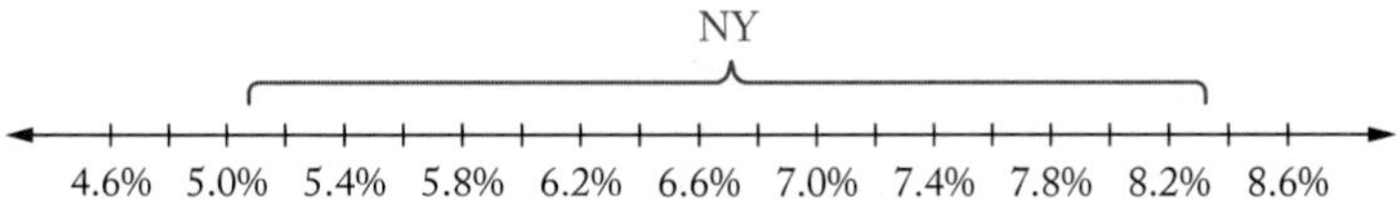

NY

4.6% 5.0% 5.4% 5.8% 6.2% 6.6% 7.0% 7.4% 7.8% 8.2% 8.6%

may wander. For example, in January 2007, the unemployment rate was 4.3 percent and in March 2010, it was 8.7 percent. It is simply the average distance the unemployment rate wanders.

We can produce a similar picture of New York's unemployment rate (Figure 18). Here, we see that New York's unemployment rate wandered an average of 1.6 percentage points away from New York's 6.7 percent average.

Finally, if we compare the unemployment rates in the two states—accounting for both the average and the standard deviation—we get a picture like that in Figure 19.

Note that the two ranges almost entirely overlap. While the average unemployment rates in the two states are different, when we examine both the averages and the standard deviations, we see that the unemployment rates in the two states wandered over very similar ranges. Looking at this last picture, we would be more likely to conclude that there isn't much of a difference in unemployment rates across the two states.

Figure 19
Average and Standard Deviation of
Unemployment Rates in New York and Pennsylvania

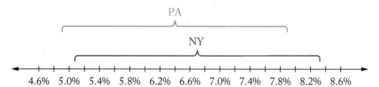

Conversely, compare Pennsylvania's and California's unemployment rates (Figure 20). California's average unemployment rate over the period 2005 through 2015 was 8.4 percent—two percentage points higher than Pennsylvania's. And when we look at both the standard deviations and the averages, we see that Pennsylvania's unemployment rate did (on average) wander over an area that included the wanderings of California's

Figure 20
Average and Standard Deviation of
Unemployment Rates in California and Pennsylvania

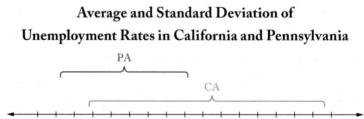

unemployment rate. But, California's unemployment rate also wandered over a large range that Pennsylvania's did not.

Consequently, we would be less likely to conclude that Pennsylvania's and California's unemployment rates were similar than we would that Pennsylvania's and New York's were similar.

The preceding explanation is a simplified description of the correct procedure for comparing two data sets. When performing comparisons like these, statisticians use what are called **p-values** to determine whether the two averages are the same. The p-value is a measure, based on the observed averages and standard deviations, of the probability that the two averages are, in fact, the same.[37] The p-value for the comparison of Pennsylvania's unemployment rate to New York's is 0.139. For simplicity, we can translate the result this way: "There is a 13.9 percent chance that the apparent difference we see between Pennsylvania's and New York's unemployment is due to random chance."[38] The p-value for the comparison of Pennsylvania's unemployment rate to California's is 0.000.[39] We can translate this as meaning that there is virtually no chance that the apparent difference we see between Pennsylvania's and California's unemployment rates is due to random chance.[40]

71

But if two states' average unemployment rates differ, why should we care whether they differ only because of random chance? We care because differences that are due to random chance won't persist over time, but differences that are not due to random chance will. For example, suppose you flip a fair coin five times and get five heads. Because the coin is fair, you know that it was simply random chance that you got five heads in a row. Therefore, you won't expect to get another five heads if you flip the coin five more times. But if you flip a weighted coin five times and get five heads, because you know the coin is weighted, you also know that those five heads weren't due to random chance. And because they weren't attributable to random chance, you will expect to get five more heads if you flip the coin five more times. The same principle applies to the unemployment rates. If the difference between Pennsylvania's and New York's unemployment rates is due to random chance, then we would not expect to observe the difference in the future. Conversely, if the difference between Pennsylvania's and California's unemployment rates is not due to random chance, then we would expect to continue to observe the difference in the future.[41]

Comparing Income Inequalities

An argument sometimes levied against free markets is that, without the government controlling the economy, the rich

can exploit the poor and corporations can monopolize indus-
tries, thereby taking advantage of consumers and workers.[42]
The result, so the argument goes, will be increased income
inequality. We can attempt to address this concern by divid-
ing the countries of the world into two groups: those with
more free markets and those with less free markets.

We'll use the Fraser Institute's Economic Freedom of the
World Index.[43] Each year, Fraser looks at the degree of government control in a country's markets by measuring things
such as the fraction of spending controlled by government,
the level of taxation, the progressivity of taxation, the magnitude of welfare programs, and other factors. Fraser then combines these measurements into a single number—a "freedom
index"—that represents the degree of economic freedom in
the country. A higher score (on a scale of 1 to 10) indicates
a greater degree of economic freedom. One factor Fraser
does not consider in creating the freedom index is income
inequality.

Let us take the 116 reporting countries and look at (picking a round number) the 50 that ranked highest for economic
freedom and the 50 that ranked lowest. We'll leave out the
middle 16 countries because, being in the middle, they are
likely to be more similar to each other than either to the 50
more free countries or to the 50 less free countries. For each

country, the Central Intelligence Agency reports a measure of income inequality called the **Gini coefficient**.[44] The Gini coefficient ranges from 0 (perfect income equality—i.e., each person has the same income) to 100 (perfect income inequality—i.e., one person has all the income and the rest have nothing). The Gini coefficients for the countries are shown in Figure 21 (called a **bar chart**).

Figure 21 demonstrates the problem of comparing stochastic variables. Some countries on the left show less inequality than do some countries on the right, and vice versa. A proper

Figure 21
Freedom Index Gini Coefficients

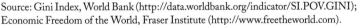

Source: Gini Index, World Bank (http://data.worldbank.org/indicator/SI.POV.GINI); Economic Freedom of the World, Fraser Institute (http://www.freetheworld.com).

comparison of the less economically free countries with the more economically free countries requires that we know the average and standard deviation of each group. The Gini coefficients in the less economically free countries average 42.5 with a standard deviation of 7.5. The Gini coefficients in the more economically free countries average 35.8 with a standard deviation of 9.4. The p-value for the difference in the two averages is 0.0002. That is well below the typical cutoff of 0.05.[45] Therefore, we conclude that the difference in the average Ginis across the two groups is likely not due to random chance.

This **difference of means test** doesn't tell us anything about causality. It is possible that increased economic freedom causes less inequality. It is possible that less inequality causes more economic freedom. It is also possible that increased economic freedom and less inequality are jointly caused by something else. What the test does tell us is that, whatever the causality, the differences in average Gini coefficients we observed—one group with an average 42.5 and the other with an average 35.8—are likely due to something other than random chance.

The ultimate purpose of statistical analysis is to enable us to predict or influence the future. For example, we want to understand the relationship between economic freedom and peace because we'd like more peace, and if economic freedom yields more peace, then perhaps we should encourage more economic freedom. We want to know whether the probability of dying is greater in a Boeing or in a Concorde because we want fewer people to die. We want to know who pays the most taxes because we want to adjust tax rates so that everyone pays a fair share. We want to know whether unemployment is greater in Pennsylvania or in California because we want to know where we have a better chance of starting a successful business. Comparing stochastic measures such as fatality rates, tax rates, and unemployment rates is a first step in using statistics to make decisions. The next step is finding relationships among various stochastic measures.

4

How Do We Know When One Thing Affects Another?

More sophisticated than simply comparing the magnitudes of two variables is asking whether *changes* in one variable are related to *changes* in another variable. Comparing averages only tells us whether one variable is (on average) larger than the other. A more sophisticated procedure, called **regression analysis,** tells us how much one variable changes as another changes.

Suppose we want to know the relationship between a car's speed and the driver's reaction. For simplicity, let's assume that it takes the driver one second to react to an event.

For example, if a ball bounces into the street, one second elapses between the time the ball comes into view and when the driver depresses the brake. If the car is traveling 20 miles per hour (mph), then during that one second, the car will travel 29 feet. That's about two car lengths. If the car is traveling 40 mph, then the car will have traveled 59 feet by the time the driver hits the brakes. This relationship between the car's speed and how far it will travel before the driver hits the brakes is shown in Figure 22.

We can also represent the line in Figure 22 as an equation:

$$\text{Distance Traveled} = 1.467 \times \text{Speed}$$

Figure 22

Regression Analysis: Distance Traveled at Various Speeds

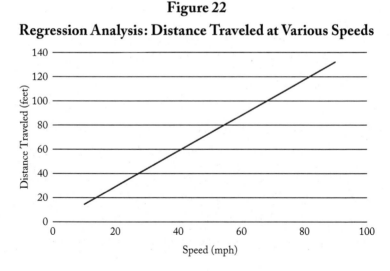

We call this a **regression equation**. The graph is better for providing a visually intuitive representation of the relationship. The equation is better as a tool for performing calculations concerning the relationship. But both communicate the same thing: the relationship between speed and distance.

We built the relationship shown in Figure 22 on the assumption that it takes the driver one second to react. In reality, it takes drivers different times to react depending on what else is going on in the car and on the road, how tired the driver is, and many other factors. Suppose we repeat the analysis, but this time instead of assuming that it takes the driver one second to react, we use an actual driver and measure his reaction time.

Figure 23 shows the actual distance a car travels between the time a real driver sees the ball and when he hits the brakes. Notice that the dots aren't arranged in a neat line as they are in Figure 22. That's because, for many reasons, a real driver doesn't react in exactly one second every single time. Sometimes his reaction time is faster and sometimes it is slower. Figure 23 shows two things. First is the average trend. The trend (depicted by the straight line—called a trend line or regression line) is the underlying relationship between the driver's speed and distance traveled, on average. Second are deviations from the trend. Those are shown by the

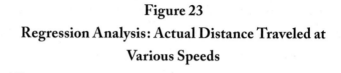

Figure 23

Regression Analysis: Actual Distance Traveled at Various Speeds

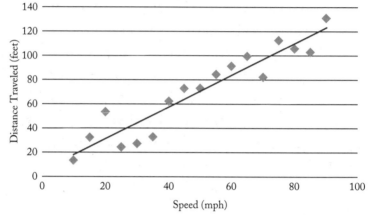

distance between the dots and the line. For example, when the driver was going 60 mph, he reacted slower than, on average, he reacted at other speeds. We know this because the dot at 60 mph is above the trend line, indicating that it took the driver longer than expected to react. When the driver was going 80 mph, he reacted faster than, on average, he did at other speeds. We know this because the dot at 80 mph is below the trend line.

Regression analysis takes data like that shown in Figure 23 and divides it into two parts: a deterministic component and a stochastic component. The deterministic component, as represented by the trend line, shows the average relationship between two variables. The stochastic component, as represented by deviations of individual data points from the trend line, shows the influence of random events on the relationship.

The regression equation that accompanies Figure 23 is

$$\text{Distance} = 1.483 \times \text{Speed} + u$$

The first part of the equation (Distance = 1.483 × Speed) is the deterministic portion of the relationship and corresponds to the regression line. The deterministic portion tells us the average relationship between the driver's speed and reaction time. For example, according to this equation, if the driver is traveling at 30 mph, we can expect (on average) the driver to travel 1.483 × 30 = 44.49 feet between the time he sees the ball and the time he hits the brakes. Now, while this is what we can expect on average, we know that random events will cause the driver's actual reaction time to deviate from the average. Sometimes he'll stop more quickly and sometimes more slowly. This random component is represented by u in the regression equation. This term, called the **error term**, represents the random deviations of the dots from the line. The purpose of regression analysis is to take data composed of both deterministic and stochastic components and to filter out the stochastic component. With the stochastic component filtered out, what's left is the underlying deterministic relationship.

For example, let's compare economic freedom and gender inequality. For each country, the United Nations Development Programme compares women's earnings, life expectancies, and educations with those of men and produces a gender inequality index. The gender inequality index ranges from 0 to 1. A value of 0 indicates that, for a given country, the quality of life for the average women is equal to that of the average man. A higher gender inequality index indicates that the quality of life for the average woman is not equal to that of the average man. The United Nations does not consider economic freedom when constructing its gender inequality index, and the Fraser Institute does not consider gender inequality when constructing its economic freedom index. So, if economic freedom is unrelated to gender inequality, the data should show no relationship. A simple comparison of averages shows that countries that are more economically free (those on the right side of Figure 24) have a lower average gender inequality index than do countries that are less economically free (those on the left side).

All that Figure 24 tells us is that less free countries experience more gender inequality and more free countries

Figure 24

Average Gender Inequality and Average Economic Freedom

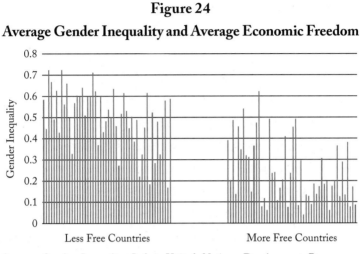

Source: Gender Inequality Index, United Nations Development Programme (http://hdr.undp.org/en/content/gender-inequality-index-gii); Economic Freedom of the World, Fraser Institute (http://www.freetheworld.com).

experience less gender inequality. A more interesting question is, "By how much does gender inequality fall as economic freedom rises?" This question is not about the magnitudes of the variables, but about the relationship between them. Specifically, we want to know what the relationship is between gender inequality and economic freedom.

Simple Regression

Regression analysis quantifies the relationship by first assuming that whatever relationship might exist between gender inequality and economic freedom is **linear**.[46] The equation takes this form:

Gender Inequality = a + b (Economic Freedom) + u

where a and b are numbers that we'll estimate using the data, and u is a placeholder that represents all factors other than economic freedom that influence gender inequality. The error term, u, captures all the randomness that exists in the relationship between inequality and freedom. If the relationship between inequality and freedom were deterministic (like the relationship between air speed and air pressure), then the error term would always be zero. If there was no relationship between inequality and freedom, then b would be zero, and the relationship would be driven entirely by the error term. In other words, the relationship would be completely random. We call this **simple regression** because we are showing Gender Inequality as a function of only one thing—Economic Freedom.

To see how regression analysis works, let's first look at the data. If we measure the economic freedom data on the horizontal axis and the gender inequality data on the vertical axis, we get Figure 25 (called a **scatter plot**).

The scatter plot in Figure 25 provides more information than the bar chart in Figure 24. The bar chart simply shows

Figure 25
Gender Inequality vs. Economic Freedom Index,
1995–2011

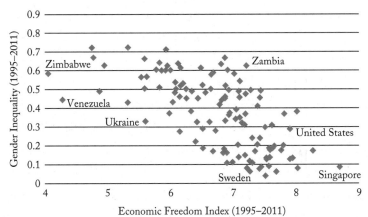

Source: Gender Inequality Index, United Nations Development Programme (http://hdr.undp.org/en/content/gender-inequality-index-gii); Economic Freedom of the World, Fraser Institute (http://www.freetheworld.com).

the countries in order of economic freedom—those with less economic freedom on the left, and those with more on the right. The height of the bars represents the degree of gender inequality present in each country. What the bar chart doesn't tell us is by how much inequality changes with a change in economic freedom.

The scatter plot improves on the bar chart by comparing both the degree of gender inequality and the amount of economic freedom in each country. In the scatter plot in Figure 25, each dot represents a country. The dot's horizontal location indicates the country's economic freedom measure (further to the right is "more free," further to the left is "less free"), and its vertical location indicates the country's gender inequality measure (further up is "less equal," further down is "more equal").

The scatter plot illustrates the important difference between an *anecdote* and a *trend*. Compare Zambia and Ukraine. Zambia experiences more economic freedom than Ukraine and it suffers more gender inequality than Ukraine. If we were to rely on anecdotes, we might point to these two countries as examples that economic freedom yields gender inequality. But, since the relationship between economic freedom and gender inequality is (at least in part) due to random events, we would be wrong in drawing such a conclusion from only two data points. With only two data points, we have no way of knowing whether the difference we see is due to something deterministic or to something stochastic. Instead, if we step back and look at all the dots at the same time, we see a pattern. On average, the dots fall as you move from the top left to the bottom right of the graph.

In Figure 26, the straight line that approximates the data is called a **trend line** or a **regression line**. We obtain the line

Figure 26
Trend Line: Gender Inequality Compared with Economic Freedom Index, 1995–2011

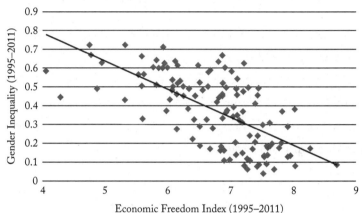

Source: Gender Inequality Index, United Nations Development Programme (http://hdr.undp.org/en/content/gender-inequality-index-gii); Economic Freedom of the World, Fraser Institute (http://www.freetheworld.com).

by selecting *a* and *b* in the earlier equation so that (roughly speaking) the line comes as close as possible to as many dots as possible while remaining a straight line.[47]

For this data set, the values of *a* and *b* that cause the line to come closest to the most dots are $a = 1.38$ and $b = -0.15$. These values are determined by statistical formulas complicated enough to require a computer or statistical calculator (and therefore beyond the scope of this discussion).

Regression involves two steps. First, we assume that the relationship between two data sets is linear:

Gender Inequality = $a + b$ (Economic Freedom) + u

The variable on the left (Gender Inequality) is called the **outcome variable**. The variables on the right (there may be more than one, though here we have Economic Freedom only) are called **factor variables**.[48] We use a statistical algorithm to estimate values for a and b. This gives us the **estimated regression equation**:

$$\text{Estimated Gender Inequality} =$$
$$1.38 - 0.15 \text{ (Economic Freedom)}$$

Notice two things. First, the error term, u, has disappeared in the estimated regression equation. Second, we have replaced "Gender Inequality" with "Estimated Gender Inequality." The u term represents all things other than Economic Freedom that influence Gender Inequality. When we estimate the regression equation, we filter out those other influences. What remains is the relationship between Economic Freedom and what Gender Inequality *would be* if the other influences were not present. We call this Estimated Gender Inequality.

For example, consider the four countries in Table 4, each of which has an Economic Freedom index of 6.15.

Table 4. Economic Freedom and Gender Inequality, 1995–2011, Four Examples

Country	Economic Freedom	Gender Inequality
Iran	6.15	0.46
Vietnam	6.15	0.27
Bolivia	6.15	0.52
Mauritania	6.15	0.61

Source: Gender Inequality Index, United Nations Development Programme (http://hdr.undp.org/en/content/gender-inequality-index-gii); Economic Freedom of the World, Fraser Institute (http://www.freetheworld.com).

The table also gives each country's Gender Inequality measure. Even though the countries all have the same Economic Freedom index, their Gender Inequality measures differ because Economic Freedom is not the only factor that influences Gender Inequality. Those other factors are part of the error term, u, in the regression equation.

If we plug the countries' Economic Freedom index into our estimated regression equation, we get:

$$\text{Estimated Gender Inequality} = 1.38 - 0.15 \times 6.15 = 0.46$$

Our regression analysis says that, after filtering out the effects of things other than Economic Freedom, we should expect each of these four countries to have a Gender Inequality of 0.46. That is, we *estimate* that Gender Inequality should

Table 5. Economic Freedom, Gender Inequality, Estimated Gender Inequality, and Residual, 1995–2011

Country	Economic Freedom	Gender Inequality	Residual
Iran	6.15	0.46	0.00
Vietnam	6.15	0.27	0.19
Bolivia	6.15	0.52	−0.06
Mauritania	6.15	0.61	−0.15

Source: Gender Inequality Index, United Nations Development Programme (http://hdr.undp.org/en/content/gender-inequality-index-gii); Economic Freedom of the World, Fraser Institute (http://www.freetheworld.com).

be 0.46 when Economic Freedom is 6.15. The difference between the Gender Inequality and the Estimated Gender Inequality is an estimate of the regression error (called the **residual**). The residual, shown in Table 5, is the difference between the Gender Inequality we observed and the portion of Gender Inequality we estimate is attributable to Economic Freedom.

We now know enough to talk about the nature of the relationship between our outcome and factor variables. There are three parts to the relationship: **significance**, **magnitude**, and **precision**. The significance of the relationship indicates the likelihood that the apparent relationship between two variables is deterministic rather than stochastic.[49] The magnitude of the relationship indicates by how much one variable changes when another changes. The precision indicates the proportion of variation in the values of a variable that can be explained by the variations in the values of other variables.

For example, consider the relationship between air pressure and the diameter of the container holding the air. In a balloon, the internal air pressure and the balloon's diameter move together (Figure 27). We say that the pressure/diameter relationship is significant: the diameter rises with air pressure not because of random chance but because of deterministic physical properties. The same is true for the air pressure in

Figure 27
A Balloon Expanding

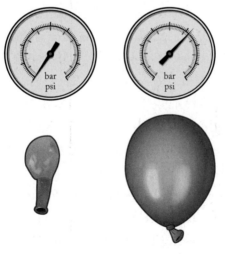

a tire and the tire's diameter. However, a given increase in a tire's air pressure will result in a much smaller diameter increase than will the same increase in a balloon's air pressure. Although both relationships are significant, the *magnitude* of the pressure/diameter relationship in the tire is small while the magnitude in the balloon is large. The fact that the balloon's diameter changes by a large amount while the tire's changes by a small amount is attributable to differences in the materials used to make each and to the thickness of the walls of each. These additional factors—material composition and wall thickness—also affect the diameter and so reduce the precision of the pressure/diameter relationship.

A useful tool for describing precision, or how closely the estimated regression equation fits the data, is the R^2 (pronounced "R-squared" and also called the **squared multiple correlation coefficient**). R^2 measures what fraction of variations in the outcome variable is explained by variations in the factor variables. For the data in Figure 26, the R^2 is 0.44, meaning that 44 percent of the variation in Gender Inequality can be attributed to variations in Economic Freedom.

Upon seeing the scatter plot in Figure 26, people who know a little bit about statistics might ask, "What's the R^2?" They are thinking that a low R^2 means that the relationship between Economic Freedom and Gender Inequality isn't significant. That is not a correct interpretation of R^2. The measure of the significance of the relationship between Economic Freedom and Gender Inequality is the p-value. A lower p-value indicates a stronger relationship. The rule of thumb is that p-values less than 0.05 indicate a relationship strong enough to be noteworthy. For our data set, the p-value is 0.000, indicating a highly significant relationship between Economic Freedom and Gender Inequality.[50]

The R^2 measures the precision of the relationship. For our data set, 44 percent of the variation in Gender Inequality can be attributed to variations in Economic Freedom. That means the remainder, 56 percent of the variation in Gender Inequality, is due to factors we have not considered in our equation. Finally, the value of the coefficient (also called the **slope**, or **slope coefficient**) attached to Economic Freedom, -0.15 in the estimated regression equation, measures the magnitude of the effect of Economic Freedom on Gender Inequality. On average, a one unit increase in Economic Freedom is associated with a 0.15 unit decline in Gender Inequality. (See Table 6.)

To remember the difference between significance (p-value), magnitude (coefficient value), and precision (R^2), consider the following analogy. You and your friend are at a party. You are on one side of a crowded room and your friend is on the

Table 6. Relationship Attributes

Relationship Attribute	Description	Statistic[a]
Significance	The likelihood that an apparent relationship between variables is deterministic.	p-value
Magnitude	The amount by which one variable changes when another changes.	Slope coefficient
Precision	The proportion of variation in the outcome that can be explained by variations in the factors.	R^2

[a]A lower p-value indicates greater significance. A higher (in absolute value) slope coefficient indicates greater magnitude. A higher R^2 indicates greater precision.

other side. You yell to your friend, "Help me find my phone!" The reason you yell the words is to attempt to elicit help. That is, you are attempting to establish a relationship between your words and your friend's actions. We can use what we know about significance, magnitude, and precision to describe this relationship.

Because the room is crowded and noisy, your friend hears not just your voice but also the voices of everyone else in the room. Of all the sound that reaches your friend's ear, the percentage that comes from your voice—the precision—is measured by R^2. The more quiet the other people in the room are compared to you, the higher the R^2 is. The more noisy the other people in the room are compared to you, the lower the R^2 is. Just because your friend can hear your voice, doesn't mean that he can make out what you are saying. The extent to which your friend can not just hear your voice but also can make out the words you are saying—the significance—is measured by the p-value. The better able your friend is to make out your specific words, the lower the p-value is. The less able your friend is to make out what you are saying, the higher the p-value is. Finally, the fact that your friend hears your voice and understands your words doesn't mean that your friend is going to get up and help you find your phone. The extent to which your words spur your friend to action—the magnitude—is measured by the slope coefficient. The less apt your friend is to take action in response to your plea, the closer to zero is the slope coefficient.

All three attributes of a statistical relationship are important, though for different reasons. If you want to know whether smoking reduces your life expectancy, you care about the significance (the p-value) of the relationship between smoking and longevity. If you want to know by how much your life expectancy declines on average when you smoke one more cigarette per day, you care about the magnitude (the slope coefficient) of the relationship. If you want to know how much of your life expectancy is due to smoking versus other life choices, you care about the precision of the relationship (the R^2).

Multiple Regression

We use multiple regression to estimate the relationship between an outcome variable and more than one factor variable. The benefit of multiple regression is that it can filter out the effects of multiple factor variables simultaneously. For example, suppose you are responsible for scheduling trucks for a trucking company. Each truck is an expensive piece of equipment, so you don't want trucks sitting idle. On the other hand, when a customer calls you asking you to make a delivery, you need to be able to tell the customer when you'll have a truck available. To schedule the trucks well, you need to be able to predict how long each truck will be gone making deliveries. How long a truck is gone depends on many things: the weather, traffic conditions, how far the truck has to travel, how many stops the truck needs to make, driver skills, and so on. Suppose that you have data on two of these things: how many miles a truck needs to travel (roundtrip) to make its deliveries and how many stops it will need to make to unload deliveries. You've recorded this data along with how long the trucks were gone (Table 7).

Table 7. Truck Scheduling

Travel Time (Hours)	Miles Traveled	Stops
11.3	500	4
6.8	250	3
10.9	500	4
8.5	500	2
6.2	250	2
8.2	400	2
9.4	375	3
8.0	325	4
9.6	450	3
8.1	450	2

You will be sending a truck to make two stops. Roundtrip, it will travel 325 miles. You need to estimate how long the truck will be gone. How do you do this?

One reasonable approach is to notice that the trucks in your data set logged 87 hours total travel time, 4,000 total miles, and 29 total stops. On average, your trucks take 0.022 hours per mile and 3 hours per stop.

$$\text{Average hours per mile} = \frac{87 \text{ hours}}{4{,}000 \text{ miles}} = 0.022 \text{ hours per mile}$$

$$\text{Average hours per stop} = \frac{87 \text{ hours}}{29 \text{ stops}} = 3 \text{ hours per stop}$$

If your trucks average 0.022 hours per mile, then a truck traveling 325 miles should be gone $0.022 \times 325 = 7.15$ hours. That seems straightforward. Of course, this ignores the stops. If your trucks average 3 hours per stop, then a truck making two stops should be gone $3 \times 2 = 6$ hours. But, that ignores miles traveled. We could combine the two measures. If a truck traveling 325 miles should be gone 7.15 hours and a truck making two stops should be gone 6 hours, then a truck that travels 325 miles and makes two stops should be gone $7.15 + 6 = 13.15$ hours. But, this doesn't seem right either. It could be that the more stops a truck makes, the more miles it would have to travel. If this were true, then adding the two numbers would double count the effects of miles and stops on time. We could average the two numbers (7.15 hours and 6 hours) to get 6.58 hours, but that seems arbitrary.

Notice the problem. It is not clear how we should handle these two pieces of information: hours per mile, and hours per stop. If we use only one of the measures, we unrealistically ignore the other. But if we add them together, we get a number that may be inflated because of double counting, and averaging them seems arbitrary. The underlying problem isn't simply that one set of averages underestimates and another overestimates. The problem is that the averages aren't even measuring what we want to know. What we want to know is not the average number of hours it takes to make a stop and the average number of hours it takes to travel a mile, but how much time an additional stop or an additional mile will add to the truck's time away. These things sound similar, but they can be very different.

For example, suppose it takes one hour to make one dozen cookies. That's an average of 5 minutes per cookie. How long would it take to make two dozen cookies? If we look at the average measure of 5 minutes per cookie, we'd conclude that two dozen cookies should take two hours. But clearly that's not right. It might take a little longer to make two dozen cookies than to make one dozen, but it won't take *twice* as long. If you're already making one dozen cookies you don't then start over again from the beginning for the second dozen. If you can, you make all two dozen cookies in one batch. What we want to know is not the average time it takes to make a dozen cookies, but the *extra* time required to make an *additional* dozen cookies. The extra time required to bake one more cookie is called the **marginal effect** of a cookie on time. The average time required to bake all the cookies is called the **average effect** of cookies on time. Average effects look backward by showing the combined effect of many occurrences of a factor (cookies) on an outcome (time). Marginal effects look forward by

99

showing the effect of one more occurrence of a factor on the outcome.

To find the marginal effect of miles on time and the marginal effect of stops on time, we need to filter out the effect of miles on time from the effect of hours on time. Multiple regression does this. We can combine our three measures into a single regression equation:

$$\text{Time} = a + b\,(\text{Miles}) + c\,(\text{Stops}) + u$$

Time is the variable we are attempting to explain, so it is the outcome variable. We are using Miles and Stops to explain Time, so Miles and Stops are factor variables. Feeding the data into statistical software generates the following estimated regression equation:

$$\text{Estimated Time} = 1.13 + 0.01\,(\text{Miles}) + 0.92\,(\text{Stops})$$

The R^2 for the estimated regression line is 0.90. That means variations in Miles and Stops (together) account for 90 percent of the variations in Time. The remaining 10 percent of the variation in Time is due to things other than Miles and Stops—for example, variations in traffic conditions, weather conditions, and so forth. The slope coefficient for Miles has a p-value of 0.000.[51] The slope coefficient for Stops has a *p*-value of 0.004. Both of these are well below the 0.05 cutoff, so we would conclude that both Miles and Stops have significant effects on Time.

Finally, look at the magnitude of the slope coefficients. In a multiple regression equation, the slope coefficients are the marginal effects. That means they show the effect of one factor on the outcome after filtering out the effects of the other factors on the outcome. For example, the results tell us that each additional stop adds 0.92 hours to the travel time *after* accounting for the effect of miles on travel time. Similarly, each additional mile traveled adds 0.01 hours to the travel time *after* accounting for the effect of stops on travel time.

Our goal was to predict the travel time for a truck traveling 325 miles and making two stops. Using our estimated regression equation, we have our estimate:

$$\text{Estimated Time} = 1.13 + 0.01 \times 325 + 0.92 \times 2 = 6.22 \text{ hours}$$

The multiple regression equation accounts for both the effect of miles on time and the effect of stops on time but filters out overlap in the two effects so that there is no double counting.

But what about that 1.13? That is the estimate for *a*, which is called the **intercept**. The intercept is the time we expect a truck to be gone that travels zero miles and makes zero stops. Here is the equation:

$$\text{Estimated Time} = 1.13 + 0.01 \times 0 + 0.92 \times 0 = 1.13 \text{ hours}$$

But a truck that travels no miles and makes no stops doesn't make sense. How do we interpret this calculation? It turns out that 1.13 is a fixed time that is independent of miles or stops. Think of it as "overhead"—a constant amount of time that is common to all trips, regardless of the number of miles or stops. For example, before setting out on each trip the driver may need to check the oil in his engine, the air pressure in his tires, and that the load is securely strapped down. All of those activities eat up time even though the truck has traveled no miles and made no stops. The intercept measures this overhead.

Experimentation and Control

In a laboratory setting, botanists test for the effects of chemicals on plants by growing two groups of identical plants under (nearly) identical conditions, with just one deliberately chosen exception. One group of plants is exposed to a chemical and the other is not. If all other conditions (water, air, temperature, sunlight, etc.) are the same for the two groups of plants

HOW DO WE KNOW WHEN ONE THING AFFECTS ANOTHER?

and the plants that are exposed to the chemical die, then the botanists can conclude that the chemical is poisonous to the plants.

Where humans are involved, controlled experimentation is often not possible. But we can use multiple regression in an attempt to mimic the effects of controlled experimentation. Because a multiple regression filters out the effects of factors on the outcome, if we have enough observations, we can obtain results similar to those from controlled experimentation.

For example, suppose we want to know whether differences in tax rates across counties in the United States encourage people to move. Three reasonable arguments can be made. First, people may want to avoid high tax rates, and to that end move out of counties with higher tax rates into counties with lower tax rates. Second, people may desire the government services that can be provided with more tax revenue, in which case they will tend to move out of counties with lower tax rates and into counties with higher tax rates. Third, tax rates may be relatively unimportant, and people may base their decisions about moving on other factors, such as employment prospects, climate, and crime.

We cannot conduct a laboratory experiment because we cannot control extraneous factors that might influence people's decisions, such as employment, climate, and crime. Even if we could, unlike the plants, people aren't the same. Some people will care more about crime than taxes. Some people will care more about taxes than climate. Some people will care more about employment than crime. Multiple regression solves these problems by filtering out the effects of extraneous factors and filtering out random differences in individuals.

One such study looked at the relationship between the top marginal income tax rate and the number of high-income households (households with annual incomes of $200,000 or more) as a fraction of all households.[52] Suppose the authors estimated this regression equation:

$$\text{High-Income Households} = a + b \, (\text{Top income tax rate}) + u$$

Suppose they found a significant negative relationship between the top income tax rate and the number of high-income households. That is, they found that when the income tax rate was higher, there were fewer high-income households. Does that mean high-income households are avoiding high-tax counties? Possibly. But such a finding would raise reasonable questions. It *could* be that the income tax rate affected the number of high-income households. But it could also be that high-income households and the income tax rate were *both* affected by some other unseen factor. For example, counties with colder climates might need higher taxes to pay for road maintenance. Meanwhile, high-income households can afford to live wherever they want and may choose to live in warmer climates. In this example, the income tax rate may have no effect on the number of high-income households. But because both variables are affected by the weather, the two *appear* to be related in the data.

If we could conduct a controlled experiment, we would place high-income households in two counties that were in every way identical except that one county had a higher income tax and the other had a lower income tax, and then we'd watch to see how many of the high-income households moved between the two counties. But because we can't impose experimental controls, we are left open to criticisms like the "cold climate" argument discussed earlier.

Multiple regression comes to the rescue by statistically factoring out the effects of the factors we can't control. The authors in the study of high-income households estimated the following multiple regression model:

$$
\begin{aligned}
\text{Number of High-Income Households} = a + \\
b \, (\text{Top income tax rate}) + c \, (\text{Top income bracket cutoff}) \\
+ d \, (\text{Property tax rate}) + e \, (\text{Sales tax rate}) \\
+ f \, (\text{Unemployment rate}) + g \, (\text{Crime rate}) \\
+ h \, (\text{Mean temperature}) + u
\end{aligned}
$$

The results from this more complicated regression model show the relationship between the top income tax rate and the number of high-income households *after* filtering out the effects of income bracket definitions, property taxes, sales taxes, unemployment, crime, and the average temperature on the number of high-income households. After filtering out the effects of all of those things, the data still showed that higher income tax rates were associated with lower numbers of high-income households.

We've seen how probabilities, comparisons of averages and standard deviations, and regression can be used to give us insights into stochastic relationships—insights that can't be seen by looking at specific examples. But understanding statistical results is contingent on understanding the measures that feed into the statistical results. A statistical result such as "cats, on average, are larger than dogs" doesn't ring true if by "dogs" and "cats" we mean domesticated dogs and cats. But it makes more sense if by "dogs" and "cats" we mean undomesticated dogs and cats (e.g., wolves, foxes, lions, and tigers). The definitions of the stochastic variables become very important in understanding the nature of particular stochastic relationships.

What Do Economic
Measures Tell Us?

The media often quote economic statistics: GDP, unemployment, inflation. But most people who know what these terms mean aren't aware of important nuances. For example, as discussed earlier, unemployment is not the opposite of employment. The existence of a third category, nonemployment, means it is possible for the unemployment rate to fall and yet for more people to be out of work. Nuances like this can result in people misinterpreting the information that these economic statistics provide.

Measuring Production

Gross domestic product (**GDP**) is the most frequently cited measure of the strength of an economy. We associate a rising

GDP with more employment and higher incomes. When economists and politicians talk about economic stimulation or the economy slowing down, they are usually talking about changes in GDP. GDP measures the market value of all **final goods and services** produced in a country in a given year. By "final," economists mean goods and services that are not used in the production of other goods and services. For example, when you buy a car for your personal use or electricity for your home, you are purchasing a final good or service. But a cleaning service that purchases a car to transport its employees and cleaning supplies, or a business that purchases electricity to run its machinery or light its office, has purchased **intermediate goods**. Whether a good or service is "final" or "intermediate" depends on the use to which it is put.

The reason GDP ignores intermediate products is that counting them would result in double counting of production. For example, suppose a car manufacturer spends $30,000 on labor, materials, energy, overhead, and other factors producing a car that it sells for $31,000 to a dealer. The manufacturer took $30,000 worth of inputs and transformed them into output worth $31,000. How do we know the output is worth $31,000? We know because someone (the dealer) willingly paid $31,000 for it. The manufacturer took $30,000 worth of inputs and added $1,000 worth of value. Suppose the dealer then sells the car to a consumer for $33,000. The dealer took something worth $31,000 and transformed it (by providing transportation from the factory, storage until purchased, and help to the consumer in choosing which car to buy, and completing the paperwork) into something worth $33,000. The dealer added $2,000 worth of value. When we add to GDP the $33,000 the consumer paid for the car, we are capturing the value added at each stage in the production process going all the way back to the raw materials. The values of the final goods include the values of all the inputs that went into bringing the final goods to the consumer.

GDP excludes a significant amount of production, largely because the production can't be measured. Work people do at home—cutting their grass, cleaning their homes, washing their cars, watching their kids—is productive work. It should be included in GDP. The fact that people are doing these things for themselves or their families is irrelevant; they are nonetheless producing goods and services. However, because no money changes hands, the value of these goods and services can't be measured and included in GDP. GDP is calculated from tax and payroll records. If no money changes hands, no record is generated. For the same reason, the production of illegal goods and services (e.g., recreational drugs) is excluded, as is the illegal production of otherwise legal goods and services (e.g., work done "under the table").

The point of GDP is to measure production within a country, so goods and services produced outside the country are not counted. And because the purpose is to measure production, money that changes hands for reasons other than production isn't counted either. For example, transfer payments (money the government gives to people) and purchases of stocks and bonds don't represent production and so aren't included in GDP.

So, GDP does not count all economic activity, just economic activity involving final products. The assumption is that increased economic activity in final products implies increased economic activity up the supply chain. An alternate measure, **gross output (GO)**, counts sales of both final and intermediate goods and services. Because of double counting, GO isn't useful for measuring the total value of goods and services an economy produces, but it is more useful than GDP for measuring economic activity because it measures all sales in the economy.

A larger problem with both measures is that they don't distinguish between a dollar spent on apple pies and a dollar spent on mud pies. For example, politicians are quick to point out that GDP rises when the government spends more money. But that is true merely by definition. It ignores the fact that when GDP rises because of government spending, the additional goods and services produced are goods and services that politicians and bureaucrats have selected, whereas when GDP rises because of private spending, the additional goods and services produced are goods and services that consumers have selected. In other words, GDP counts a billion dollars of smart phones as being equivalent to a billion dollars of smart bombs. But the former tends to generate far more consumer satisfaction than the latter.

In the end, we can say in very general terms that an increase in GDP (or GO) indicates that the economy is expanding. Often, but not always, that's good: it can be good if it means that people are producing more things that people want. But it can be bad if the things being produced are things we'd rather not have. For example, a decline in energy prices will spur an increase in GDP as it becomes cheaper to produce and transport goods. That increase in GDP is good because it means that people can buy more things they want and, generally, buy them at lower prices. But government spending on a war will also spur an increase in GDP as businesses ramp up production of goods for the war effort. Putting aside the noneconomic circumstances surrounding the war, this increase in GDP isn't good because the economy is producing more things that people would rather not have (such as more tanks and fighter aircraft) in exchange for fewer things people would rather have (such as more cars and commercial aircraft).

Measuring Quality of Life

Both GDP and GO measure sales. But people's quality of life is influenced by more than simply what they buy. Health and longevity matter, as does education. Poverty matters and, at least in some instances, inequality matters. The United Nations Development Programme (UNDP) compiles several indices that attempt to measure quality of life across countries. Chief among them is the Human Development Index (HDI).[53] The UNDP combines measures of income, education, and longevity and assigns each country an HDI that ranges from 0 (extremely low quality of life) to 1 (extremely high quality of life). Figure 28 shows the HDIs for 2013.

In 2013, HDIs ranged from a low of 0.34 for Niger to a high of 0.94 for Norway. In general, European countries appear to score higher on the HDI—the lowest is Bulgaria at 0.78. But many non-European countries score better than Bulgaria, including Libya, Uruguay, and Cuba. In fact, more than half of the countries with HDIs in the range of 0.78 and 0.94—the

Figure 28
Human Development Index, 2013

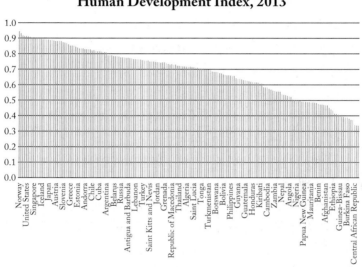

Source: United Nations Development Programme, "Human Development Index" (http://hdr.undp.org/en/content/human-development-index-hdi).

low and high for European countries—aren't European countries. This point raises a statistical question: Do European countries score better on the HDI than non-European countries? The question is simple to ask but not simple to answer because there is no "European" HDI nor a "non-European" HDI. Some individual European HDIs are greater than some individual non-European HDIs and vice versa. The HDIs are stochastic across countries, so we can only compare the two sets statistically. The average HDI for the European countries is 0.87; for non-European countries it's 0.65. These two averages are statistically different with a p-value of 0.000.[54] In English, that means the observed difference in the two averages is likely not the result of random chance. Thus, we can conclude that, though the individual countries vary, the average for the European countries is greater and by an amount likely not due to random chance.

GDP (per capita) and HDI measures give us a sense of the living standards of the average person, but they don't necessarily tell us anything about the poor. A separate measure, the poverty rate, tells us that. There are several major poverty measures from which to choose: some measure the fraction of the population living on less than a specified amount of money; others measure the fraction of the population consuming less than a certain amount of food. The charts that follow show the poverty rates for the 76 countries for which we have data for at least one year over the period 2001–2010. Figure 29 shows the average poverty rate for the quarter of countries that are most economically free, the next most free quarter of countries, the next to the least free, and the least free quarter of countries. Notice that the average poverty rate is greater for the less-free countries.

Figure 29
National Poverty Rates, in Quartiles by Economic Freedom

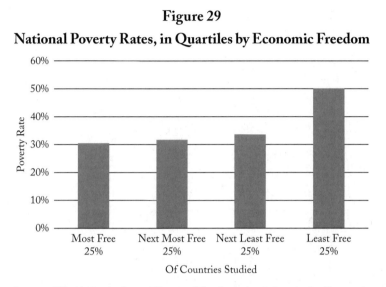

Source: World Bank (http://data.worldbank.org/topic/poverty); Economic Freedom of the World, Fraser Institute (http://www.freetheworld.com).

A different view of the same data set is presented in Figure 30. Rather than grouping the countries into four categories, this chart shows each individual country's economic freedom plotted against the country's poverty rate. Notice that the dots (on average) move down and to the right. This indicates that (on average) countries that score higher on the economic freedom index also experience less poverty.

Another statistic related to poverty is infant mortality. Generally speaking, countries with better health care experience

Figure 30
National Poverty Rates and Economic Freedom Index

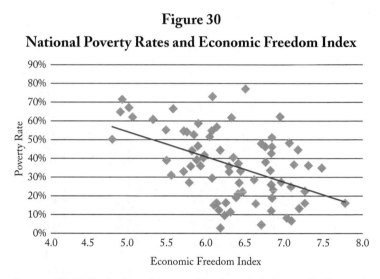

Source: World Bank (http://data.worldbank.org/topic/poverty); Economic Freedom of the World, Fraser Institute (http://www.freetheworld.com).

lower infant mortality rates. Proponents of nationalized health care point to the higher than usual infant mortality rates in the United States (compared with other developed countries) as evidence that the United States would benefit from a nationalized health care system. There are two problems with this claim. First, infant mortality is defined very differently across countries. Even among developed countries, some countries do not include in their mortality statistics infants who do not survive for a specified period beyond birth. By contrast, the United States counts all infants who, at the moment of birth, show any signs of life.[55] This difference alone would tend to cause the United States' infant mortality figures to be higher. But there is also an interesting counterforce at play in the statistics. Women in the United States tend to receive excellent prenatal care. That means sickly babies who would otherwise die *in utero* have a greater chance of surviving to birth. But babies who die *in utero* are not included in infant mortality statistics. Therefore, excellent prenatal care has the effect of putting upward pressure on infant mortality statistics.

Related to poverty measures are exploitation measures. A society that exploits the weak and discriminates against minorities imposes a lesser quality of life on its people, regardless of its average income or poverty rate. Although many peoples have been exploited and subject to discrimination over many centuries and in many cultures, two demographic groups stand out for the frequency with which they are targeted: women and children.

Again, it is interesting to compare these outcomes with economic freedom. Figure 31 shows child labor rates for the 74 reporting countries over the period 2000–2009, broken down by economic freedom (the middle 34 countries are omitted).

Figure 31
Child Labor Rates in Least and Most Economically Free Countries, 2000–2009

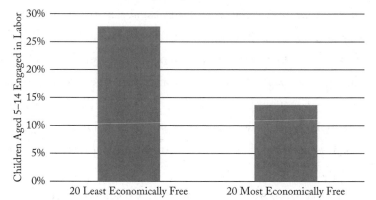

Source: Childinfo.org, UNICEF; Economic Freedom of the World, Fraser Institute.

The chart shows that the average child labor rate was almost twice as high among the 20 least economically free countries as among the 20 most economically free. A reasonable counterargument can be made to this result. People in rich countries have the leisure to be concerned with and fight for economic freedom. Also, people in rich countries don't like to see their children exploited. Therefore, it is possible that the result we see in the chart is due to the "rich country effect." That is, there is no relationship between economic freedom and child labor. Economic freedom and child labor rates are actually both correlated with a third, unseen, factor: wealth.

One way to address this criticism is to repeat the analysis but look only at the poorest countries. It is possible that, among the poorest countries, the relationship actually reverses. If economically free countries tend to have fewer labor restrictions, they may be more likely to tolerate child labor. The data are shown in Figure 32 (the middle five countries are removed).

Figure 32
Child Labor Rates in Poorest Countries, 2000–2009

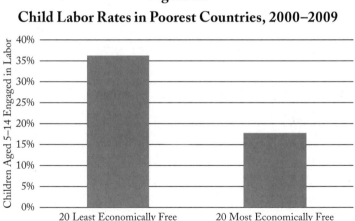

Source: UNICEF (http://data.unicef.org/topic/child-protection/child-labour/); Economic Freedom of the World, Fraser Institute (http://www.freetheworld.com).

119

We see the same pattern emerge. Of course, by developed countries' standards, the child labor rates are unacceptably high in both cases. Despite this, the pattern persists: economically free poor countries have lower child labor rates than do economically unfree poor countries.

Conclusion

Anecdotes catch our imaginations and stick in our memories. Perhaps humans evolved to embrace anecdotes because one's neighbors' experiences helped one avoid possibly fatal errors from eating the wrong plant or hunting the wrong animal. Humans dressed up their anecdotes with colorful details and even created artificial anecdotes to entertain and educate. These became the first stories handed down from one person to the next. As modern humans, we retain our primal thirst for anecdotes, and it is this urge that drives our multibillion-dollar entertainment industry. Although anecdotes give us a colorful and entertaining view of the world around us, that view is often murky. Good decisions are best made with far more clear, though less colorful, statistics. The drawback is that statistics are creatures of mathematics.

To make practical use of them, we translate what they tell us into English. And therein lies the danger of our coloring into them meanings or nuances that they don't possess.

The trick to understanding statistics is to put aside deterministic thinking—to stop thinking in terms of anecdotes and start thinking in terms of aggregates. Deterministic, nonrandom, truths hold for every instance—that iron has a higher melting temperature than aluminum is true for every example of iron and aluminum. A statistical truth does not necessarily hold in every instance. It exists in the intersections among the instances. It is statistically true that an increase in the price of gas causes people to drive less. Not every person will drive less when the price of gas rises, but the effect of those who do drive less will outweigh the effect of those who drive more. In the aggregate, people will drive less.

Understanding statistics is the first step toward seeing the world more clearly. For simplicity, we talk as if the world were nonrandom. We say things like, "Smoking will kill you," and "Practice improves performance." In describing the world in nonrandom terms, we forget that important randomness exists everywhere. The truth is that smoking won't kill you, but it will increase the probability of your dying at a younger age. Practice does not improve performance, but it does increase the probability of better performance. Acknowledging randomness helps us make better decisions by encouraging us not to look to specific examples for direction but to look for statistical patterns in many examples to extrapolate underlying truth.

Endnotes

1. Branko Milanovi, "True World Income Distribution, 1988 and 1993: First Calculations, Based on Household Surveys Alone," World Bank Development Research Group Working Paper no. 2244, 1999.

2. John Allen Paulos, *Innumeracy: Mathematical Illiteracy and Its Consequences* (Dumfries, NC: Holt McDougal, 2001).

3. It is possible for two phenomena, X and Y, to be uncorrelated and yet causally related, but the conditions are rare. It requires that a third unaccounted variable, W, be both highly negatively (positively) correlated with X, and have an impact on Y that is of the same magnitude and same (opposite) sign as the marginal impact of X on Y. For example, suppose we examine data on rainfall and an outdoor plant's growth and find no correlation. The claim that absence of correlation implies absence of causation suggests that rainfall does not cause the plant to grow—which is clearly incorrect. However, the only way to observe data like these would be for someone to act in such a way that the plant received the same amount of water regardless of whether it rained, watering the plant only when it didn't rain and ensuring that the amount of water the person provided was the same as the amount of water the plant received when it did rain.

4. The original data show weekly earnings. Those weekly earnings are multiplied by 52 in Figure 6 to show the earnings on an annualized basis.

5. The original data are grouped for ages 16–19, 20–24, 25–34, 35–44, and 45–54, which produces a step function. The data in Figure 6 are interpolated to form a smooth progression within each age group.

6. Economic Mobility Project, "Economic Mobility of the States," Pew Center on the States, Washington, 2012. Figures are in 2006 dollars.

7. The Census Bureau defines a person as "looking for work" if the person is a civilian, aged 16 or older, and at some point within the previous four weeks registered at an employment office, met with a prospective employer, investigated possibilities for starting a business, answered a job advertisement or placed an advertisement requesting a job, applied for a job, or is an active member of a union (https://www.census.gov/people/laborforce/about/acs_employ.html).

8. There are multiple measures of the unemployment rate, called U1 through U6. Each successive measure is broader than the previous one. The commonly cited "unemployment rate" (and the one used in this example) is actually U3.

9. Gallup.com, "U.S. Economic Confidence Index (Weekly)," http://www.gallup.com/poll/125735/economic-confidence-index.aspx.

10. Bureau of Labor Statistics, "Consumer Price Index," http://www.bls.gov/cpi/cpifaq.htm.

11. These numbers are as of January 2016. As additional data come in, more recent CPI figures will be revised slightly.

12. $(236.71 - 232.96) / 232.96 = 0.016$.

13. CoinNews Media Group, "U.S. Inflation Calculator," http://www.usinflationcalculator.com/inflation/consumer-price-index-and-annual-percent-changes-from-1913-to-2008/.

14. U.S. Energy Information Administration, "Petroleum and Other Liquids," http://www.eia.gov/dnav/pet/hist/LeafHandler.ashx?n=pet&s=emm_epm0_pte_nus_dpg&f=a; Statista, "Average Selling Price of Desktop PCs Worldwide from 2005 to 2015," http://www.statista.com/statistics/203759/average-selling-price-of-desktop-pcs-worldwide/.

126

ENDNOTES

15. Federal Housing Finance Agency, "Federal House Price Index Rises for 13th Consecutive Quarter," News Release, November 25, 2014, p. 3, http://www.fhfa .gov/AboutUs/Reports/ReportDocuments/HPI%203Q%202014.pdf.

16. Government Accountability Office, "Financial Audit: U.S. Government's Fiscal Years 2015 and 2014 Consolidated Financial Statements," February 25, 2016, http:// www.gao.gov/assets/680/675425.pdf; https://obamawhitehouse.archives.gov/omb /budget/Historicals.

17. Antony Davies, "3 Lies about Jobs and the Unemployment Rate" *USNews*, May 29, 2012.

18. National Center for Health Statistics, Centers for Disease Control and Prevention, "Accidents or Unintentional Injuries," http://www.cdc.gov/nchs/fastats /accidental-injury.htm.

19. National Transportation Safety Board, "Aviation Accident Database and Synopses," http://www.ntsb.gov/_layouts/ntsb.aviation/index.aspx.

20. Leighton Walter Kille, "Transportation Safety over Time: Cars, Trains, Planes, Walking, Cycling," *Journalist's Resource*, October 5, 2014, http://journalists resource.org/studies/environment/transportation/comparing-fatality-risks -united-states-transportation-across-modes-time.

21. Federal Bureau of Investigation Criminal Justice Information Services Division, "Murder Victims, by Weapon, 2007–2011," *Crime in the United States, 2011*, https://www.fbi.gov/about-us/cjis/ucr/crime-in-the-u.s/2011/crime-in-the -u.s.-2011/tables/expanded-homicide-data-table-8.

22. The figures here ignore government transfers—money the government gives to people (e.g., Earned Income Tax Credits). If we include government transfers in the calculations, the top 1 percent pay an average effective rate of about 29 percent, the middle 20 percent pay an average effective rate of around *negative* 11 percent, and the poorest 20 percent pay an average effective rate of *negative* 55 percent. Including government transfers, the bottom 60 percent of taxpayers receive back from the federal government more than they pay in.

127

23. Bart K. Holland, *What Are the Chances? Voodoo Deaths, Office Gossip, and Other Adventures in Probability* (Baltimore, MD: Johns Hopkins University Press, 2002).

24. Ken Manktelow, *Thinking and Reasoning: An Introduction to the Psychology of Reason, Judgment and Decision Making* (New York: Psychology Press, 2012).

25. $(0.062 - 0.042) / 0.042 = 0.48$

26. $72 / 1,200 = 0.06$

27. $288 / 1,200 = 0.24$

28. $288 / 960 = 0.3$

29. $72 / 240 = 0.3$

30. The ages are determined by the *New England Journal of Medicine* study on suicides among Accutane users. Suicide numbers for the general population prior to 1999 are only available for ages 10 through 34.

31. The total population is the average for the age group over the years 1982 through 2000.

32. $37 / 5,000,000 = 0.000007 = 0.0007\%$

33. $34,337 / 13,700,000 = 0.00251 = 0.251\%$

34. The analysis shown here is simplified for demonstration. Complications arise due to distinguishing between Accutane users who used the drug for a short while and those who were on the drug for a longer duration. Additional complications arise due to distinguishing between younger and older users. Those who are interested can review the more complex analysis published in the *New England Journal of Medicine*.

35. *Stanford Encyclopedia of Philosophy*, http://plato.stanford.edu/entries/paradox -simpson.

36. In this example, the systemic portion of the unemployment rate is properly called the **population mean.** Combining the systemic and stochastic portions gives us what is called the **sample mean.**

ENDNOTES

37. Technically speaking, the *p*-value is the probability of our observing the sample data we have observed when, in fact, the two population averages are identical.

38. For a non-statistician, this is an adequate interpretation of a *p*-value. The technically correct interpretation is less intuitive: "If the systemic portions of Pennsylvania's and New York's unemployment rates were the same, there would be a 13.9 percent chance of observing the sample data we did observe."

39. The first nonzero digit occurs beyond the third decimal place.

40. The rule of thumb is to conclude that two averages are different if the *p*-value falls below 0.05.

41. Assuming, of course, that there are no major alterations to economic conditions in the two states.

42. For more in-depth discussion of this topic, see Antony Davies, James R. Harrigan, and Megan Teague, "Equality, Liberty, and Prosperity," *Social Philosophy and Policy* 31, no. 2 (2015): 180–203.

43. Fraser Institute, "Economic Freedom World Rankings, 2014," http://www.freetheworld.com.

44. Central Intelligence Agency, "Distribution of Family Income: Gini Index," *The World Factbook*, https://www.cia.gov/library/publications/the-world-factbook/rankorder/2172rank.html.

45. In many disciplines, including economics, the accepted cutoff for *p*-values is 0.05. A *p*-value above 0.05 is taken to mean that there is no compelling evidence that the observed difference between the two groups is due to anything other than random chance. A *p*-value below 0.05 is taken to mean that there is compelling evidence that the observed difference is not due to random chance. Some studies use a more restrictive cutoff of 0.01. The *p*-value shown here indicates compelling evidence, even under this more restrictive cutoff, that the difference in inequalities is not due to random chance.

46. A linear relationship is one that, when graphed, yields a straight line.

47. This is an intuitive explanation only. In fact, the values for *a* and *b* are selected so as to minimize what's called the "sum of the squared residuals." What that is and how the procedure is performed are subjects for statistical analysis.

48. The outcome variable is also known as the **dependent**, or **endogenous** variable. The factor variables are also known as **independent, explanatory,** or **exogenous** variables. The terms aren't perfect synonyms, but the distinctions among them involve statistical nuances that go beyond the discussion here.

49. This is an imperfect but perhaps more intuitively appealing description. The correct description is less intuitive: "significance" is the inverse of the probability of observing two variables moving together when, in fact, there is no deterministic relationship between them.

50. The first nonzero digit occurs beyond the third decimal place.

51. The first nonzero digit occurs beyond the third decimal place.

52. Antony Davies and John Pulito, "Tax Rates and Migration," Mercatus Center Working Paper no. 11-31, August 2011. The study looked at the 791 counties in the United States with populations of 65,000 or more over the period 2004–2009.

53. United Nations Development Programme, "Human Development Index," http://hdr.undp.org/en/content/human-development-index-hdi.

54. The first nonzero digit occurs beyond the third decimal place.

55. Scott W. Atlas, "Critics of U.S. Health Care Disseminate Misinformation Cloaked as Data" *National Review*, September 14, 2011.

Recommended Readings

Antony Davies, James R. Harrigan, and Megan Teague, *"Equality, Liberty, Prosperity."* Written for non-statisticians, "Equality, Liberty, Prosperity" takes a statistical view of the relationship between more versus less restrictive economic policies and socioeconomic outcomes such as income, poverty, inequality, and population growth. The article asks whether differing levels of government control of economies across states and across time is associated with differing quality-of-life outcomes. This article is a good follow-up to this book for people who are interested in the application of statistical analysis to social and economic questions. The article is available in *Social Philosophy and Policy*, Volume 31, Issue 2, or at http://www.antolin-davies.com/research/elp.pdf.

Murray R. Spiegel and Larry J. Stephens, *Schaum's Outline of Statistics,* **and John J. Schiller, R. Alu Srinivasan, and Murray R. Spiegel,** *Schaum's Outline of Probability and Statistics.* The *Schaum's Outline* series can be used as references or read as books. These provide a good first step for people looking to learn how to compute statistics in addition to understanding what statistics tell us.

Damodar N. Gujarati and Dawn C. Porter, *Basic Econometrics.* In many fields, regression analysis is the foundation of the most complex statistical analysis. Gujarati and Porter's book is more mathematically heavy than the other works in this list but provides a good introduction to regression analysis.

About the Author

Antony Davies is associate professor of economics at Duquesne University. Dr. Davies authors regular columns on economics and public policy for the *Philadelphia Inquirer* and *U.S. News & World Report* and cohosts *Words and Numbers*, a weekly podcast on economics and policy. He has written hundreds of op-eds for, among others, the *Wall Street Journal, Los Angeles Times, New York Daily News, Washington Post,* and *Huffington Post*. In addition to his academic work, Dr. Davies was associate producer at the Moving Pictures Institute and chief financial officer at Parabon Computation, founded several technology companies, and is cofounder and chief academic officer at FreedomTrust, a nonprofit educational institution. Dr. Davies earned his BS in economics from Saint Vincent College and PhD in economics from the State University of New York at Albany.

Index

Note: Page numbers with f, t, or n indicate figures, tables, and endnotes, respectively.

Libertarianism.org

Liberty. It's a simple idea and the linchpin of a complex system of values and practices: justice, prosperity, responsibility, toleration, cooperation, and peace. Many people believe that liberty is the core political value of modern civilization itself, the one that gives substance and form to all the other values of social life. They're called libertarians.

Libertarianism.org is the Cato Institute's treasury of resources about the theory and history of liberty. The book you're holding is a small part of what Libertarianism.org has to offer. In addition to hosting classic texts by historical libertarian figures and original articles from modern-day thinkers, Libertarianism.org publishes podcasts, videos, online introductory courses, and books on a variety of topics within the libertarian tradition.

Cato Institute

Founded in 1977, the Cato Institute is a public policy research foundation dedicated to broadening the parameters of policy debate to allow consideration of more options that are consistent with the principles of limited government, individual liberty, and peace. To that end, the Institute strives to achieve greater involvement of the intelligent, concerned lay public in questions of policy and the proper role of government.

The Institute is named for *Cato's Letters*, libertarian pamphlets that were widely read in the American Colonies in the early 18th century and played a major role in laying the philosophical foundation for the American Revolution.

Despite the achievement of the nation's Founders, today virtually no aspect of life is free from government encroachment. A pervasive intolerance for individual rights is shown by government's arbitrary intrusions into private economic transactions and its disregard for civil liberties. And while freedom around the globe has notably increased in the past several decades, many countries have moved in the opposite direction, and most governments still do not respect or safeguard the wide range of civil and economic liberties.

To address those issues, the Cato Institute undertakes an extensive publications program on the complete spectrum of policy issues. Books, monographs, and shorter studies are commissioned to examine the federal budget, Social Security, regulation, military spending, international trade, and myriad other issues. Major policy conferences are held throughout the year, from which papers are published thrice yearly in the *Cato Journal*. The Institute also publishes the quarterly magazine *Regulation*.

In order to maintain its independence, the Cato Institute accepts no government funding. Contributions are received from foundations, corporations, and individuals, and other revenue is generated from the sale of publications. The Institute is a nonprofit, tax-exempt, educational foundation under Section 501(c)3 of the Internal Revenue Code.

CATO INSTITUTE
1000 Massachusetts Ave., N.W.
Washington, D.C. 20001
www.cato.org